THE YOUNG ADULT'S GUIDE TO
SCHOOL FUNDRAISING

101 Fun & Easy Ideas for
Big Events

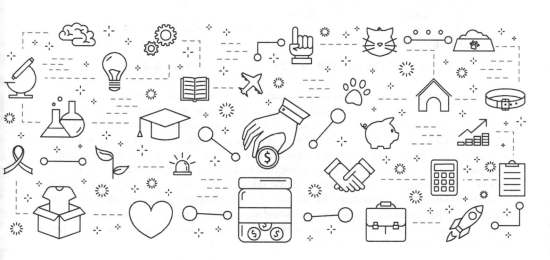

By Atlantic Publishing Group Staff

THE YOUNG ADULT'S GUIDE TO SCHOOL FUNDRAISING: 101 FUN & EASY IDEAS FOR BIG EVENTS

Copyright © 2018 Atlantic Publishing Group, Inc.

1405 SW 6th Avenue • Ocala, Florida 34471 • Phone 800-814-1132 • Fax 352-622-1875
Website: www.atlantic-pub.com • Email: sales@atlantic-pub.com
SAN Number: 268-1250

Library of Congress Cataloging-in-Publication Data

Names: Atlantic Publishing Group.
Title: The young adults guide to ... school fundraising 101 : fun & easy ideas for big events / by Atlantic Publishing Group, Inc.
Other titles: School fundraising 101 : fun & easy ideas for big events.
Description: Ocala, Florida : Atlantic Publishing Group, Inc., [2018] | Audience: Grades 9-12. | Includes bibliographical references and index.
Identifiers: LCCN 2018023872 (print) | LCCN 2018028596 (ebook) | ISBN 9781620231661 (ebook) | ISBN 9781620232330 | ISBN 9781620232330?(library edition :?alk. paper) | ISBN 9781620231654?(pbk. :?alk. paper)
Subjects: LCSH: Fund raising—Juvenile literature.
Classification: LCC HV41.2 (ebook) | LCC HV41.2 .Y68 2018 (print) | DDC 658.15/224—dc23
LC record available at https://lccn.loc.gov/2018023872

Printed in the United States

PROJECT MANAGER: Danielle Lieneman
INTERIOR LAYOUT: Nicole Sturk

Reduce. Reuse. RECYCLE.

A decade ago, Atlantic Publishing signed the Green Press Initiative. These guidelines promote environmentally friendly practices, such as using recycled stock and vegetable-based inks, avoiding waste, choosing energy-efficient resources, and promoting a no-pulping policy. We now use 100-percent recycled stock on all our books. The results: in one year, switching to post-consumer recycled stock saved 24 mature trees, 5,000 gallons of water, the equivalent of the total energy used for one home in a year, and the equivalent of the greenhouse gases from one car driven for a year.

Over the years, we have adopted a number of dogs from rescues and shelters. First there was Bear and after he passed, Ginger and Scout. Now, we have Kira, another rescue. They have brought immense joy and love not just into our lives, but into the lives of all who met them.

We want you to know a portion of the profits of this book will be donated in Bear, Ginger and Scout's memory to local animal shelters, parks, conservation organizations, and other individuals and nonprofit organizations in need of assistance.

– Douglas & Sherri Brown,
President & Vice-President of Atlantic Publishing

Table of Contents

Food and Drink

Games and Contests

Holidays and Special Occasions

Shows

Sports

Themed Events

Miscellaneous

Introduction

I f you are a member of a nonprofit organization, such as a theatre troupe, sports team, or marching band, you know there are countless reasons to fundraise. From the need to travel for a competition to buying new uniforms or other equipment, fundraising is a great way to support these endeavors. With increased budget cuts to schools, there has been a loss of investment in extracurricular activities and programs, making fundraising even more essential.

This book provides a ideas for planning and executing your next big fundraiser to finance your school, nonprofit, church group, or other organizational ventures.

Each idea includes its relative costs, preparation needed, and other factors that can help you determine find the perfect fundraising event for your organization's needs. Relative costs are conveyed using a one to five $ system where $ represents a low cost event while $ $ $ $ $ is a high-cost event. An additional one- to five-star rating is assigned to other factors, such as finding volunteers, a venue, sponsors, and the planning and execution of the event. One star signifies a relatively easy task, while a five-star task is harder to accomplish.

Specific details about what else is needed for each event are also included, such as unique equipment and number of volunteers needed. A list of potential sponsors and donors is provided. Don't discount the power of social media to self-promote your event either; Facebook events and other social media tools are a great, free way to get the word out about your event.

There are online resources and success stories throughout the book to show how organizations have already taken these ideas and successfully met their fundraising goals.

Remember, it is important to be realistic about your monetary target, but don't be discouraged before you have even started. Even if you feel uncomfortable asking members of your community for money, know that many of them want to contribute and help you towards your goals. Those who cannot help by donating will often offer their services in the form of volunteering or otherwise.

Rationale behind the ratings

★	The fundraiser is very easy or costs little to nothing.
★ ★	While still easy to do, events with this ranking need slightly more work, planning or money to pull off.
★ ★ ★	A moderate amount of work or money is necessary. You may have to find volunteers who are willing and able to sell somewhat expensive products or tickets. You may have to book a venue, which is at least moderately challenging.
★ ★ ★ ★	There is more than the average amount of time, effort, or funds required.
★ ★ ★ ★ ★	The event is somewhat difficult or expensive. It may require a lot of preparation or hands-on work. It may require a lot of materials or resources.

Auctions and Raffles

Auctions can be a great way to raise a lot of money, but they are also a lot of work. It takes time and effort to solicit donations, and hosting an auction is a major event that requires significant planning and volunteer help.

Planning

Give yourself at least six months to plan the event, even up to a year if possible. Planning a major event is similar to planning a big wedding — you need a venue, decorations, entertainment, food and beverages, and a guest list.

Sponsors

Consider asking a business to sponsor the entire event. Know what you can promise them. Offer to include their name or logo on event materials or link to their social media. Remember to further thank your sponsors during the actual event.

Volunteers

For most auctions, you'll need at least 10 volunteers from your group, including leaders of committees for food, decorations, sponsors, advertising, ticket sales, and setup/cleanup. You'll want as many people as possible to sell tickets to the event. Be sure to assign enough volunteers to the setup and cleanup committees.

For a live auction, consider asking a professional auctioneer to donate his or her services.

Venue

Nice hotels are great places for these kinds of events because they offer large ballrooms that accommodate many people as well as catering, sound systems, and lighting, but your school's auditorium would work just fine.

Preparation

Start off by putting together a committee to make decisions about the auction and delegate work to. Then move on to deciding the type of auction, deciding a venue, sponsors, and fundraising goals.

Be confident when asking for donations or sponsorships, and be clear in what you are fundraising for; this will make possible sponsors more inclined to help your cause. From there you can move on to advertising the event to the community using social media, radio commercials, newspaper ads, flyers posted around busy areas of town, and other means. If you can, decide a target audience and cater to these people. It is more effective to directly appeal to a certain audience than trying to encompass the blanket term of 'everyone.' Target audiences can be based on almost anything, but age and location are easy to market to.

Always arrive early to set up the event, and account for time needed to break down and clean up the venue afterwards. For planned activities during the event, consider creating a script for the master of ceremonies to read. Be transparent about the items offered in the event, and do not advertise items that won't be sold or that you cannot guarantee will be sold on auction day. Ideally wait until you have several items and business sponsorships before advertising to the community.

1. Bachelor Auction

Description: Invite single male firefighters, police officers, athletes, and other eligible bachelors to volunteer to impress female bidders with their style and charm. The highest bidders will have photos taken with the bachelors, as well as share refreshments and a dance with them.

Estimated Cost:

Levels of Difficulty:

Obtaining Sponsors/Donations	✪ ✪ ✪
Finding a Venue	✪ ✪
Recruiting Volunteers	✪ ✪
Preparation	✪ ✪ ✪
Execution	✪ ✪ ✪

Special Materials/Equipment:

☐ Stage

☐ Sound system (speakers, microphone)

Sponsor/Donation/Volunteer Tip(s):

- Consider asking a major supporter to sponsor the entire event.

- Invite your supporters to be table sponsors and purchase a table that seats 10 people. The sponsor can sell the tickets to friends or give them away to family or business associates.

- Assign one volunteer to greet the bachelor participants.

Execution Tip(s):

- Have volunteers there early to set up and check lighting and sound systems.

- Arrange a comfortable "green room" area for bachelors to wait.

- Have your members or volunteers sell tickets at the door.

- Have a script for the MC to follow

Variation(s):

- For additional profits, create a calendar of all the bachelors, and sell it by the entrance.

- Make it a Bachelorette Auction.

Success Story A team of volunteers organizes an annual bachelor auction in Calgary, Alberta, Canada to raise money for Survive and Thrive, a local cancer charity. In June 2017, their auction of 10 bachelors from their community raised $9,544. Read more: **https://www.facebook.com/ BachelorAuctionYYC/**

2. Blind Gift Auction

Description: Have attendees bring a wrapped gift with them to this event — the trickier the better — think big boxes for small items or heavy packaging for light contents. Because the bidder has no idea what they're bidding on, try to get a mix of valuable prizes and humorous gag gifts. The element of surprise is what makes it fun.

Estimated Cost: $ $ $

Levels of Difficulty:

Obtaining Sponsors/Donations	✪ ✪ ✪
Finding a Venue	✪ ✪
Recruiting Volunteers	✪ ✪
Preparation	✪ ✪ ✪
Execution	✪ ✪ ✪

Sponsor/Donation/Volunteer Tip(s):

- Consider asking a major supporter to sponsor the entire event.

- Invite your supporters to be table sponsors and purchase a table that seats 10 people. The sponsor can sell the tickets to friends or give away to family or business associates.

Execution Tip(s):

- Try to scatter the valuable gifts throughout the evening to hold bidders' interest.

3. Car Raffle

Description: Who wouldn't want to throw in a few bucks for a chance at winning some hot new wheels? Rev up your profits by raffling a brand-new car from a local auto dealer.

Estimated Cost:

Levels of Difficulty:

Obtaining Sponsors/Donations	★ ★ ★ ★ ★
Finding a Venue	★
Recruiting Volunteers	★
Preparation	★ ★ ★
Execution	★ ★ ★

Sponsor/Donation/Volunteer Tip(s):

- You need a car dealer to donate a vehicle or sell you a car for their cost.

- Host the drawing at the dealership and ask the dealer to donate refreshments.

Execution Tip(s):

- Because some people will not want the vehicle, consider offering a cash prize of around $10,000 to $15,000 that the winner can choose instead.

- Do the math to figure out how many tickets you need to sell to make a profit. You should sell enough tickets to rake in about three times the amount the car is worth. If you have a $50,000 car, you should sell $150,000 worth of tickets. So, if you price your tickets at $50 each, you should sell 3,000 tickets; if tickets are $20 each, you would need to sell 7,500 tickets.

• Announce the winners at a party-like event and send out a press release with the winners and prizes listed for further publicity.

Success Story   In Santa Maria, California, several local schools participate in the Support Our Schools car raffle, sponsored by five area car dealers. In 2016, they raised a total of $153,500 to be split among the schools for projects like sports uniforms and class trips.[1]

---

1. Chandler, 2016

4. Celebrity Memorabilia Auction

Description: Rack up some A-list profits by auctioning merchandise owned by celebrities.

Estimated Cost:

Levels of Difficulty:

Obtaining Sponsors/Donations	★★★★
Finding a Venue	★★
Recruiting Volunteers	★★
Preparation	★★★★
Execution	★★★

Special Materials/Equipment:

☐ Display equipment for the merchandise

Sponsor/Donation/Volunteer Tip(s):

- Put together a list of contact information for the celebrities and send out requests. In most cases, if you are soliciting items from actors, singers, or entertainment celebrities, you will be approaching a publicist or an agent.

Execution Tip(s):

- Type up as much information as you have about each item and its donor; display the info card next to the item. Bidders want to buy merchandise with unique stories.

- Be specific about what you are asking for. For example, request an item of clothing or guitar picks.

- Be sure to ask that the celebrity sign or authenticate the item.

- Rejection letters signed by celebrities can also bring in a few dollars, so don't throw those away!

Variation(s):

- Ask celebrities to create doodles or other works of art for a celebrity art auction.

5. Chair-ity Auction

Description: Auction off new or used chairs that are uniquely presented with special decorations, accessories, and enhancements. Include all types of chairs, each decorated with a unique theme.

Estimated Cost:

Levels of Difficulty:

Obtaining Sponsors/Donations	★ ★ ★
Finding a Venue	★ ★
Recruiting Volunteers	★ ★
Preparation	★ ★
Execution	★ ★

Special Materials/Equipment:

☐ Chairs

Sponsor/Donation/Volunteer Tip(s):

• Have all your members ask anyone with artistic or decorating talent to decorate and donate chairs. Brainstorm local celebrities you might ask.

• On social media, ask for chair donations and encourage donors to get creative.

Execution Tip(s):

- Photograph each winner sitting in their purchased chair, post on social media, and tag donors and bidders.

Success Story   In 2016 Ocala Marion County Association of Realtors Young Professional Network (OMCAR)'s held its 8th Annual Chair-ity event, raising $30,761 for the Boys and Girls Club. Read more: **http://www.omcar.com/events1/annual-chair-ity-event/.**

6. Decorated Tree Auction

Description: Auction off Christmas or holiday trees decorated by florists and artists in the community. Make additional profits by auctioning miniature tree centerpieces and sets of unique ornaments.

Estimated Cost:

Levels of Difficulty:

Obtaining Sponsors/Donations	★★★★
Finding a Venue	★★★★
Recruiting Volunteers	★★★★
Preparation	★★★★★
Execution	★★★★

Special Materials/Equipment:

☐ Christmas or holiday trees

☐ Tree decoration equipment

Sponsor/Donation/Volunteer Tip(s):

• Ask tree farmers and home improvement stores to donate trees. Consider asking for donations of artificial trees right after the holidays and auction them off in the fall.

• Ask stores to donate tree decorations. Again, ask right after the holidays for decorations you can use the next year.

• Ask local artists to donate their decorating services.

Execution Tip(s):

- If using real trees, find a parking lot or other outdoor space large enough to display the trees. If using artificial trees, any indoor space large enough to display the trees is good.

- Have your members volunteer to help load trees into the winning bidders' vehicles.

7. Dessert Auction

Description: Auction off gourmet desserts in a chance auction — a combination of silent auction and raffle. Supporters purchase tickets and drop them into a container next to the item they want to win. The more tickets a supporter drops into a container, the better chance the chance of winning. At the close of the auction, a ticket is drawn from each container identifying the auction winner.

Estimated Cost:

Levels of Difficulty:

Obtaining Sponsors/Donations	★ ★
Finding a Venue	★
Recruiting Volunteers	★ ★
Preparation	★ ★ ★
Execution	★ ★

Special Materials/Equipment:

☐ Display equipment for the desserts

Sponsor/Donation/Volunteer Tip(s):

• Ask bakers, bakeries, or chefs to donate specialty sweets.

Execution Tip(s):

• Make sure desserts are as fresh and top quality as possible for the event day.

- Have many volunteers available to sell tickets during the event. Encourage attendees to buy more tickets right up to the moment winners are selected.

8. Hourly House Helper Auction

Description: Auction off the services of your members to help bidders with household chores for one (or more) hour(s).

Estimated Cost:

Levels of Difficulty:

Obtaining Sponsors/Donations	★
Finding a Venue	★ ★
Recruiting Volunteers	★ ★ ★
Preparation	★ ★ ★
Execution	★ ★ ★

Sponsor/Donation/Volunteer Tip(s):

- Brainstorm with your members what tasks they are good at or will volunteer to do.

- Focus you target audience on people living in neighborhoods, and post on community social media forums to advertise the event.

Execution Tip(s):

- Clearly advertise the abilities of each volunteer as bidding starts, so attendees who have a particular chore to be done will bid more on volunteers who can handle this task.

9. Mall Auction

Description: Ask every store in the mall to donate an item to be auctioned on-site.

Estimated Cost:

Levels of Difficulty:

Obtaining Sponsors/Donations	⭐⭐⭐
Finding a Venue	⭐⭐⭐
Recruiting Volunteers	⭐⭐
Preparation	⭐⭐⭐⭐
Execution	⭐⭐⭐

Special Materials/Equipment:

☐ Display equipment for the merchandise

Sponsor/Donation/Volunteer Tip(s):

• Ask every store in the mall to donate an item and to hang auction flyers in the store or mention the auction in their own advertising.

• Encourage the donation of products from a variety of prices and consider bundling small items together in a basket prize.

• Ask the mall management to donate space for the auction to be held inside the mall.

Execution Tip(s):

- Do not advertise any item for auction until you have the item in your possession.

- Detail where each item came from to appeal to the stores donating as they may gain future customers through this event, and would be more likely to donate to you again in the future.

10. Silent Auction

Description: Beautifully presented gift baskets, art, and jewelry are highly desirable items and the silent auction format gives bidders a good look at the merchandise. Photos can cleverly present trips and gift certificates for day spa services or massages enticing bidders to battle over them as well.

Estimated Cost:

Levels of Difficulty:

Obtaining Sponsors/Donations	⭐⭐⭐
Finding a Venue	⭐⭐
Recruiting Volunteers	⭐⭐
Preparation	⭐⭐⭐⭐
Execution	⭐⭐⭐

Special Materials/Equipment:

☐ Display equipment for the merchandise

Sponsor/Donation/Volunteer Tips:

• Seek sponsor donations for big-ticket items to auction. Vacations, adventure trips (like African safaris), and other experience gifts are great. Also, try to find sponsors to donate large home electronics.

• As you seek items for auction, offer a way that the business or individual donating the item is recognized unless they ask not to be. For example, "London Theater Vacation generously donated by XYZ Travel."

- Ideally, you want to have all auction items collected before you start selling tickets to your event. Although that is not always feasible, your big-ticket items should be locked in early to generate excitement during ticket sales.

Execution Tips:

- Have a few people in place to open, monitor, and close bidding and to collect bid sheets. Periodically announce the time left to bid. Remind people at the one-minute mark.

- Once bidding has closed, collect all of the bid sheets and determine the highest bids. You can either announce the names or numbers of the winning bidders, or you can note them and place them where the bid sheets were. Have many volunteers in place to collect payment for items purchased.

Variation(s):

- Hold the auction in conjunction with a fundraising dinner.

Dances

Dances are a fun way to engage with your community while successfully fundraising. However, planning a dance can be difficult. It takes a lot of preparation to decide themes, obtain sponsors, and host the dance in an appropriate venue.

Planning

Give yourself at least six months to plan the event, even up to a year if possible. Planning a major event is like planning a big wedding — you need a venue, decorations, entertainment, food and beverages, and a guest list.

Sponsors

Consider asking a business to sponsor the entire event. Know what you can promise them. Offer to include their name or logo on event materials or link to their social media. Remember to further thank your sponsors during the actual event.

Volunteers

Dances can be held with very few volunteers or a lot of volunteers. You'll need at least 15 volunteers to manage the food and drink stations, if there are any; watch over the dance floor during the event; and direct guests at the entrance to where seating, bathrooms, and storage for their belongings can go. For more upscale events, you might want to consider enlisting trusted volunteers to serve as valets.

If hiring a DJ is not within the budget, consider asking one to volunteer their time, or delegate a pair of volunteers to learn the venue sound system, create a playlist, and be in charge of playing the music the night of the dance.

Venue

Nice hotels or women's clubs make great venues because they often offer catering and have appropriate lighting and sound systems installed. However, any school gym or auditorium will work as well.

Preparation

Start off by creating an executive committee that is responsible for major decisions about the auction and delegating work to other committees. Then move on to deciding the type of auction, deciding a venue, sponsors, and fundraising goals.

Be confident when asking for donations or sponsorships, and be clear in what you are fundraising for; this will make possible sponsors more inclined to help your cause. From there you can move on to advertising the event to the community using social media, radio commercials, newspaper ads, flyers posted around busy areas of town, and other means. If you can, decide a target audience and cater to these people. It is more effective to directly appeal to a certain audience than trying to encompass the blanket term of 'everyone.' Target audiences can be based on almost anything, but age and location are easy to market to.

Always arrive early to set up the event, and account for time needed to break down and clean up the venue afterwards. For planned activities during the event, consider creating a script for the master of ceremonies to read. Be transparent about the items offered in the event, and do not advertise items that won't be sold or that you cannot guarantee will be sold on auction day. Ideally wait until you have several items and business sponsorships before advertising to the community.

11. Fur Ball

Description: Have dog owners dress up and enjoy a date with their furry friends. Sell tickets for admission to the event, and offer fun doggy games, photo ops, and dance contests.

Estimated Cost: $ $ $ $

Levels of Difficulty:

Obtaining Sponsors/Donations	★ ★
Finding a Venue	★ ★ ★
Recruiting Volunteers	★ ★
Preparation	★ ★ ★
Execution	★ ★ ★

Special Materials/Equipment:

☐ Dance floor

☐ Tables and chairs

☐ Photography equipment

Sponsor/Donation/Volunteer Tip(s):

• Pet stores or pet supply companies are natural choices for sponsors.

Execution Tip(s):

- See if your school administration will allow pets inside the gymnasium. If not, many hotels are becoming pet-friendly and might allow you to use a ballroom.

- Have plenty of water bowls available and offer low seats or cushions for pets to relax with their owners.

- Offer both human and pet-friendly refreshments.

- Have a designated outdoor area for potty breaks and make waste bags available.

- Consider having a photo booth with on-site printing for attendees to take photos together. Consider having a photo booth company sponsor the booth or charge a small fee for photo printing in order to cover the cost and possibly further fundraise.

- Raise additional profits by setting up a gift shop with treats and accessories.

Variation(s):

- Have a Kitty Cat Ball.

12. Dance 'Til You Drop

Description: Choose a fun theme, like Rock Around the Clock, or invite dancers to select their own dances, like the twist, disco, or salsa. Dancers will seek sponsors to pledge money to your organization for each hour they remain on the dance floor.

Estimated Cost:

Levels of Difficulty:

Obtaining Sponsors/Donations	★ ★ ★
Finding a Venue	★ ★
Recruiting Volunteers	★ ★
Preparation	★ ★ ★
Execution	★ ★ ★

Special Materials/Equipment:

- ☐ Dance floor

- ☐ Tables and chairs

- ☐ Sound system (microphone, speakers)

Sponsor/Donation/Volunteer Tip(s):

- Have dancers seek sponsors to support each hour they sign up to dance in the same manner that they would for a walk-a-thon (see sample form and rules in Appendices) or charge a fee for participants to dance.

- Get a grand prize donated for the person who dances the longest. Try getting dance lessons donated by a local studio or ask a theater to donate tickets to a professional dance show.

Execution Tip(s):

- Play a variation of music, from hip-hop to classical waltz, to appeal to a wider audience.

Variation(s):

- Host a Zumba dance party and attract people of all ages to enjoy the fast-paced Latin and international fusion dance class for a fee.

13. Father-Daughter Dance

Description: As the name implies, fathers and daughters attend the dance. You can also open it up to father-figures, to be more inclusive.

Estimated Cost:

Levels of Difficulty:

Obtaining Sponsors/Donations	⭐⭐⭐
Finding a Venue	⭐⭐⭐⭐
Recruiting Volunteers	⭐⭐⭐
Preparation	⭐⭐⭐⭐
Execution	⭐⭐⭐⭐

Special Materials/Equipment:

☐ Dance floor

☐ Tables and chairs

☐ Sound system (microphone, speakers)

Sponsor/Donation/Volunteer Tip(s):

- Ask a major supporter to sponsor the entire event. Consider sponsorship to cover the cost of the venue. Seek sponsors for say, tables of 10 for dinner. The sponsor might then give the tickets to employees, friends, or family.

Execution Tip(s):

- Consider having a photo booth with on-site printing for attendees to take photos together; consider having a photo booth company sponsor the booth, or charge a small fee for photo printing in order to cover the cost and possibly further fundraise.

- Play a mixture of partner music from swing to tango so father-daughter pairings can have fun dancing to the different genres.

- Encourage your female classmates to attend and let everyone else know that their younger and older sisters are welcome!

Variation(s):

- Have a Mother-Daughter Dance

- Set a theme, such as 1980s dress

Success Story   The Ambleside School, a private school in Ocala, Florida, held its 11th annual Father Daughter Dance in 2017. Over the years, the event has become so popular they are now holding three sessions and selling about 1,500 tickets. This is their major fundraiser each year.

14. Dancing with the Stars

Description: During this formal ball, participants get to wear elaborate costumes and fancy face masks.

Estimated Cost:

Levels of Difficulty:

Obtaining Sponsors/Donations	✪ ✪ ✪
Finding a Venue	✪ ✪ ✪ ✪
Recruiting Volunteers	✪ ✪ ✪
Preparation	✪ ✪ ✪ ✪
Execution	✪ ✪ ✪ ✪

Special Materials/Equipment:

☐ Dance floor

☐ Tables and chairs

☐ Sound system (microphone, speakers)

Sponsor/Donation/Volunteer Tip(s):

- Ask a local costume or party shops sponsor the event and donating supplies for decoration and items for volunteers to wear during the event.

Execution Tip(s):

- Consider having a photo booth with on site printing for attendees take photos together, consider having a photo booth company sponsor the booth, or charge a small fee for photo printing in order to cover the cost and possibly further fundraise.

- An outdoor venue or string lights can make for attractive décor and play off of the name of the dance.

15. Masquerade Ball

Description: During this formal ball, participants get to wear elaborate costumes and fancy face masks.

Estimated Cost: $ $ $ $

Levels of Difficulty:

Obtaining Sponsors/Donations	★ ★ ★
Finding a Venue	★ ★ ★ ★
Recruiting Volunteers	★ ★ ★
Preparation	★ ★ ★ ★
Execution	★ ★ ★ ★

Special Materials/Equipment:

☐ Masquerade decorations

☐ Dance floor

☐ Tables and chairs

☐ Sound system (microphone, speakers)

Sponsor/Donation/Volunteer Tip(s):

- Ask a local costume or party shops to sponsor the event and donate supplies for decoration and items for volunteers to wear during the event.

Execution Tip(s):

- Consider having a photo booth with on site printing for attendees to take photos together; consider having a photo booth company sponsor the booth, or charge a small fee for photo printing in order to cover the cost and possibly further fundraise.

Variation(s):

- Have a themed masquerade event, such as a Monster Mash.

16. Second-Chance Prom

Description: Adults can do up prom a second time around by bringing dates and wearing their formal best, much like their high school proms from "back in the day." This adult-only event is ideal for Parent-Teacher Association (PTA) groups and will be talked about for years to come.

Estimated Cost:

Levels of Difficulty:

Obtaining Sponsors/Donations	✪ ✪ ✪
Finding a Venue	✪ ✪ ✪
Recruiting Volunteers	✪ ✪
Preparation	✪ ✪ ✪
Execution	✪ ✪

Special Materials/Equipment:

☐ Decorations

☐ Music

☐ Sound equipment (microphone, speakers)

☐ Dance floor

Sponsors/Donations:

• Ask community venues to donate a ballroom.

• Ask catering companies to donate food.

Possible Venue(s): A hotel, venue with a ballroom, or school gymnasium will do the trick.

Recommended Volunteers: 15+ including 5 to 7 committee heads to handle the venue, food, decorations, sponsors/donations, advertising, ticket sales, entertainment, setup, and cleanup

Sponsor/Donation/Volunteer Tip(s):

- To make this an authentic prom, consider casting adult volunteers in the roles of parent and teacher chaperones.

- Negotiate deals with a limo company or have the parents' children act as chauffeurs or photographers.

- Sell corsages and boutonnières leading up to the event.

Execution Tip(s):

- Consider having a photo booth with on-site printing for attendees take photos together; consider having a photo booth company sponsor the booth, or charge a small fee for photo printing in order to cover the cost and possibly further fundraise.

- Make the event kid-friendly by letting participants' children pretend to chaperone.

Variation(s):

- Come up with a creative after-prom event, like drinks at a local bar or a late-night dance on the beach.

17. Dancing through the Decades: 60s

Description: Pick a decade, for example, the '60s. Teach all the popular '60s dances, such as The Twist, The Ska, The Monkey, The Bird, and The Tighten Up at a party focused on that era. Buy a dance video demonstrating the moves for each dance so guests can follow along. With an entry fee, guests can participate in all the dancing delight, along with other activities geared toward the era, such as face painting '60s symbols like smiley faces, flowers, or peace signs.

Estimated Cost:

Levels of Difficulty:

Obtaining Sponsors/Donations	✪ ✪ ✪
Finding a Venue	✪ ✪ ✪
Recruiting Volunteers	✪ ✪
Preparation	✪ ✪ ✪
Execution	✪ ✪ ✪

Special Materials/Equipment:

- ☐ '60s decorations
- ☐ '60s music
- ☐ Sound system (speakers, microphone)
- ☐ Dance floor
- ☐ Face paint

Sponsor/Donation/Volunteer Tip(s):

- A local historical society might be a good place to begin looking for sponsorships and/or donations to use for the evening.

Execution Tip(s):

- Consider having a photo booth with on-site printing for attendees take photos together; consider having a photo booth company sponsor the booth, or charge a small fee for photo printing in order to cover the cost and possibly further fundraise.

Variation(s):

- Any era that has a specific style associated with it, such as the '50s, '60s, or 70s, is a fun variation for a party.

Food and Drink

Food and drink gatherings, picnics, or formals are always popular since people love a good meal they do not have to cook. However, this kind of event requires extra caution in food preparation and making sure all safety and courtesy measures are taken to ensure your guests have a good time.

Planning

Give yourself at least six months to plan the event, or even up to a year if possible. Planning a major event is similar to planning a big wedding — you need a venue, decorations, entertainment, food and beverages, and a guest list.

Sponsors

Consider asking a business to sponsor the entire event. Know what you can promise them. Offer to include their name or logo on event materials or link to their social media. Remember to further thank your sponsors during the actual event.

Volunteers

An ample number of volunteers may be needed to host this type of event due to the potential need of hosts and servers. You may need to have short meetings where volunteers are taught how to properly wait customers and serve food. Depending on the size crowd you expect to host, more or less than 10 volunteers could be needed.

Venue

Restaurants or cafes are natural choices of venues for this type of fundraiser. Consider and ask appropriate places around town to see if they will host onsite or sponsor your event by catering food at a different location.

Preparation

Start off by creating an executive committee that is responsible for major decisions about the auction and delegating work to other committees. Then move on to deciding the type of auction, deciding a venue, sponsors, and fundraising goals. Be confident when asking for donations or sponsorships and be clear in what you are fundraising for; this will make possible sponsors more inclined to help your cause.

From there you can move on to advertising the event to the community using social media, radio commercials, newspaper ads, flyers posted around busy areas of town, and other means. If you can, decide a target audience and cater to these people. It is more effective to directly appeal to a certain audience than trying to encompass the blanket term of 'everyone.' Target audiences can be based on almost anything, but age and location are easy to market to.

Always arrive early to set up the event, and account for time needed to break down and clean up the venue afterwards. For planned activities during the event, consider creating a script for the master of ceremonies to read. Be transparent about the items offered in the event, and do not advertise items that won't be sold or that you cannot guarantee will be sold on auction day. Ideally wait until you have several items and business sponsorships before advertising to the community.

18. Breakfast and Book Signing with Author

Description: Have a popular local author sign books and pose for photographs during a breakfast. Charge a fee for admission.

Estimated Cost:

Levels of Difficulty:

Obtaining Sponsors/Donations	✪ ✪ ✪ ✪
Finding a Venue	✪ ✪ ✪
Recruiting Volunteers	✪ ✪
Preparation	✪ ✪
Execution	✪ ✪

Sponsor/Donation/Volunteer Tip(s):

- Ask a local restaurant to donate the venue and food or ask a local independent bookstore to host the event. Make sure the venue size corresponds with the number of people you plan to attract.

- Find an author to donate his/her time as the featured guest.

- Have one of the volunteers with photography skills donate his/her time to take the event photos.

Execution Tip(s):

- Make sure the author will have everything possibly needed (a microphone, water, a comfortable seat, a podium, a pen or marker for autographs, etc.)

19. Celebrity Cookout

Description: Feature a local or national celebrity at a community cookout. Charge a high fee for general admission to the event and schedule a time guests can meet one-on-one with the celebrity.

Estimated Cost:

Levels of Difficulty:

Obtaining Sponsors/Donations	⭐⭐⭐⭐
Finding a Venue	⭐⭐
Recruiting Volunteers	⭐⭐
Preparation	⭐⭐⭐⭐
Execution	⭐⭐⭐⭐

Special Materials/Equipment:

☐ Grilling and serving supplies

Sponsor/Donation/Volunteer Tip(s):

• Find a celebrity who will agree to attend the event and find additional sponsors who correspond with the celebrity's interests. (i.e. If your celebrity is a famous author, ask a bookstore to help sponsor the event.)

• An outdoor location, such as a large park, forest preserve, or beach where you can have a picnic barbecue is ideal. However, for the sake of the celebrity, you might choose a private park/beach or less popular outdoors venue.

Execution Tip(s):

- Check out your community's food safety codes to make sure you comply with the food preparation and service requirements.

20. Chef Competition

Description: Have chefs compete to create the best dish within a time limit. Provide each chef with a box containing identical ingredients. Allow the public to purchase tickets and judge the results.

Estimated Cost:

Levels of Difficulty:

Obtaining Sponsors/Donations	★★★
Finding a Venue	★★★★
Recruiting Volunteers	★★
Preparation	★★★★
Execution	★★★★

Special Materials/Equipment:

☐ Boxes of ingredients (one per chef)

☐ Cooking utensils and tools

☐ Serving dishes

☐ Eating utensils

Sponsor/Donation/Volunteer Tip(s):

• Upscale restaurants and grocery stores are good sponsors and donors for this event.

• Get sponsors early on but wait to get the food ingredients until just before the event so everything it fresh for competition day.

Execution Tip(s):

- Make sure that all the ingredients you supply the chefs are as fresh as possible.

- Put voting cards and writing utensils at every diner's place for fast, easy voting.

- Allow your supporters to enjoy their meals before you ask that they fill out their comment cards. Do not rush this part of the event.

Variation(s):

- Promote this event for any aspiring cooks (no experience necessary) who want to try making a dish and charge the novices an entry fee.

Success Story Over 300 guests attended the 3rd Annual Cooking Up Dreams on March 31, 2017 and helped raise a record $140,000 for FSA programs. The event featured a culinary competition and delicious samplings from 13 leading local chefs and restaurants. Congratulations to Adam White of the Santa Barbara FisHouse for winning the People's Choice for its Signature Prawnton appetizer. The Judge's Award went to Peter McNee of Convivo for his Pesce Crudo—ahi and avocado on a squid ink cracker.

All the food was amazing! Read more about our featured chefs and judges.

Proceeds from Cooking Up Dreams support Family Service Agency's youth enrichment programs including Big Brothers Big Sisters, school-based counseling, and youth behavioral health—all programs targeting low-income at-risk youth who, with the help of counseling and mentors, are able to improve their personal growth and academic experience.

21. Chocolate Tasting Party

Description: Invite supporters of your organization to a party where they can indulge in a decadent variety of chocolate. Send out fun-size chocolates or personalized candy bars with your invitations to ensure a sweet response. Charge a fee for admission.

Estimated Cost:

Levels of Difficulty:

Obtaining Sponsors/Donations	⭐⭐⭐
Finding a Venue	⭐⭐
Recruiting Volunteers	⭐⭐
Preparation	⭐⭐⭐⭐
Execution	⭐⭐⭐⭐

Special Materials/Equipment:

☐ Presentation equipment and materials

☐ Chocolate

☐ Chocolate related food items

Sponsor/Donation/Volunteer Tip(s):

• A nice upscale hotel with comfortable meeting and/or banquet facilities is ideal for the venue.

• A local chocolatier, chocolate shop, or candy company could be the main sponsor.

- Research your community for local chefs and bakers that cook with chocolate. Ask these individuals to take part in your event. You can make a strong case for their involvement if you agree to compensate with publicity.

- Consider partnering with a small non-profit arts organization such as a chamber music group or jazz ensemble to perform at your event.

Execution Tip(s):

- Make sure that all the ingredients you supply the chefs are as fresh as possible.

- Have servers push around carts with the different chocolates displayed so guests can choose which deserts they try. Limit the number of chocolates each guest can request depending on the number of participants or chocolates made by the chefs. This can be regulated through tickets or tokens that guests purchase and trade for a desert.

Variation(s):

- Throw an Ice Cream Tasting Party.

22. Cooking Demonstrations

Description: Ask local chefs to perform a cooking demonstration and charge a fee for the event. If the chefs have their own cookbook, have a book signing to raise additional funds.

Estimated Cost:

Levels of Difficulty:

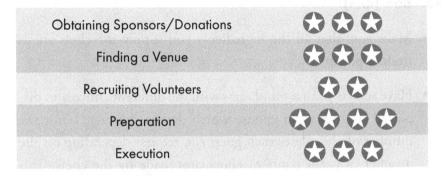

Obtaining Sponsors/Donations	★★★
Finding a Venue	★★★
Recruiting Volunteers	★★
Preparation	★★★★
Execution	★★★

Special Materials/Equipment:

☐ Food preparation and presentation supplies

Sponsor/Donation/Volunteer Tip(s):

- Seek a partnership with a local upscale restaurant with a well-known chef, if possible. The partnership will bring customers to the restaurant and may bring you a price break on the food. Ask the restaurateur if you can sell tickets through their establishment.

- Research your community for local chefs and bakers that do great things with food, and ask these individuals to take part in your event. You can make a strong case for their involvement if you agree to give them a good amount of publicity.

- Consider partnering with a small non-profit arts organization such as a chamber music group or jazz ensemble to perform at your event.

Execution Tip(s):

- If you provide the food ingredients as part of the deal, make sure all ingredients are as fresh as possible.

- If you have one, hold the book signing after the cooking demonstration, and make sure to have plenty copies of the book on hand to sell.

23. Dining with the Stars

Description: Give paying participants the opportunity of a lifetime to enjoy a meal in the company of a celebrity. The famous person could be a sports star, singer, politician, entertainer, or key leader in the community.

Estimated Cost:

Levels of Difficulty:

Obtaining Sponsors/Donations	✪✪✪✪✪
Finding a Venue	✪✪
Recruiting Volunteers	✪✪
Preparation	✪✪✪
Execution	✪✪

Sponsor/Donation/Volunteer Tip(s):

- Ask local restaurant owners to donate the dinner meals, or have a single restaurant host the event and cater

- Ask celebrities to participate and donate their time for the dinner. Have a celebrity promise to participate in the dinner before you advertise the event to the public. You can wait to advertise who the celebrity is; the mystery may encourage public interest for the event.

Execution Tip(s):

- Open the auction online through a site, such as eBay, for people to bid for a chance to win the dinner with the celebrity Only do so after a celebrity, venue, and date and time have been confirmed for the dinner.

- Once bidding ends, contact the winner and explain the arrangements of the dinner to ensure the privacy and safety of both the winner and celebrity during the dinner.

- Follow up when the event gets closer to make sure the celebrity and winner remember to attend. Make any necessary accommodations for their arrival, privacy, and comfort.

- Have a volunteer greet the celebrity and winner on the night of the dinner. Consider having a volunteer to take photos to document the special evening as well.

- Consider allowing the winner to bring a guest to make the offer more appealing.

Variation(s):

- Hold a live auction with local celebrities.

- Auction dinners prepared by celebrity chefs.

24. Exotic Meat Barbecue

Description: Give participants the chance to chew on something different. Charge for samples of wild animals, including antelope, alligator, buffalo, black bear, crocodile, iguana, ostrich, llama, and wild boar. You can plan this event like a large picnic, but with a beast of a menu.

Estimated Cost:

Levels of Difficulty:

Obtaining Sponsors/Donations	✪ ✪ ✪
Finding a Venue	✪ ✪
Recruiting Volunteers	✪ ✪
Preparation	✪ ✪ ✪ ✪
Execution	✪ ✪ ✪ ✪

Special Materials/Equipment:

- ☐ Exotic meat

- ☐ Wood and barbecue equipment

Sponsor/Donation/Volunteer Tip(s):

- Ask sporting good businesses to sponsor the event.

- Approach hunting and fishing clubs or other such social clubs and ask them to be sponsors.

- An outdoor location where meat can be barbecued on an open fire, like a large park is an ideal venue.

Execution Tip(s):

- Have volunteers act as servers and take down what guests would like to eat and relay this to the chef.

- Consider having a volunteer design a menu that can be given to the guests to look at.

25. Mocktail Party

Description: Allow people to come and enjoy a non-alcoholic, family friendly night with a great mocktail selection.

Estimated Cost: $ $ $ $

Levels of Difficulty:

Obtaining Sponsors/Donations	⭐⭐⭐
Finding a Venue	⭐⭐⭐⭐
Recruiting Volunteers	⭐⭐
Preparation	⭐⭐⭐⭐⭐
Execution	⭐⭐⭐⭐

Sponsor/Donation/Volunteer Tip(s):

- Ask a local bar or restaurant to consider hosting your mocktail party.

- Search for local bar tenders who might be able to donate their time to mixing drinks at the event or have volunteers learn to make a selection of drinks.

- Consider having other forms of entertainment, such as karaoke, live music, board games, or if the venue has space host a ping pong or similar game tournament.

Execution Tip(s):

- Have a specific selection of drinks for the menu so you can divide up funds for the ingredients easier.

- Have volunteers bring snack or finger foods to accompany the drinks for guests to enjoy.

26. Taste of the Town

Description: This food-sampling event is meant to give supporters a good taste of some of the community's top local restaurants. Community members can pay an entry fee to sample savory specialties and signature dishes prepared by local chefs.

Estimated Cost:

Levels of Difficulty:

Obtaining Sponsors/Donations	★ ★ ★ ★
Finding a Venue	★ ★ ★
Recruiting Volunteers	★ ★ ★
Preparation	★ ★ ★ ★ ★
Execution	★ ★ ★ ★ ★

Special Materials/Equipment:

☐ Cooking and serving supplies

☐ Ingredients

Sponsor/Donation/Volunteer Tip(s):

- See if your local chamber of commerce will sponsor this event, because the fundraiser may generate business for local restaurants.

- Ask restaurants to donate the time of their chefs and the ingredients of the prepared dishes. Talk to the restaurants about the free advertising they will receive with their participation. Work to get the participation of restaurants and chefs that are highly regarded. Expensive and trendy restaurants do well at events such as this. Keep in mind that people want to sample new foods, not foods they might have every day.

- Seek your local restaurant association, and/or a media company such as a local newspaper, TV or radio station to help pay for any remaining costs.

- For the venue, a large hotel with kitchen facilities and space to seat many people is best. Other options include a church, social club, or school with a kitchen and open space for tables and chairs.

Execution Tip(s):

- Have each restaurant sponsor pick one or two of the most popular items on its menu to advertise and serve at the event.

27. Thrilling Dinner Theater

Description: Offer supporters of your organization a night on the town where they can dine with the thrill of a live show happening right around their tables.

Estimated Cost:

Levels of Difficulty:

Obtaining Sponsors/Donations	★ ★ ★ ★
Finding a Venue	★ ★ ★ ★
Recruiting Volunteers	★ ★ ★
Preparation	★ ★ ★
Execution	★ ★ ★

Special Materials/Equipment:

- ☐ Costumes
- ☐ Props
- ☐ Scripts

Sponsor/Donation/Volunteer Tip(s):

- Contact a local theater group to provide performers and a script.

- You will need a location that can offer a theatrical atmosphere suitable for a dinner or the capability of handling a caterer as well as plenty of space for a performance area and an audience. An inn or a lodge is ideal, but a restaurant or club works well too.

Execution Tip(s):

- It may be fun – and earn a little more money — by having your volunteers act as wait staff for the evening.

- When you are contracting with the theater company, be sure you clarify who is responsible for paying royalties for the play that is performed.

- Your best bet is to work with a community theater. These groups are often excited by the prospect of a way to earn a little extra money and are well suited to provide the materials you need, like a good script, to make your event a success.

Variation(s):

- Increase your fundraising by coupling this event with a silent auction. Have local businesses donate auction items, and work with the theater group to offer things like singing telegrams for auction.

28. Wine Tasting

Description: Your organization can toast to a successful wine tasting with finger food, live music, dancing, and an auction. Be sure to serve many varieties of wine. As students, you are likely under the legal drinking age. Only put on this event if you have adults who can assist you.

Estimated Cost: $ $ $ $

Levels of Difficulty:

Obtaining Sponsors/Donations	★ ★ ★ ★
Finding a Venue	★ ★ ★ ★
Recruiting Volunteers	★ ★ ★
Preparation	★ ★ ★
Execution	★ ★ ★

Special Materials/Equipment:

☐ Wine

☐ Wine glasses

☐ Sound equipment (microphone, speakers)

☐ Music

☐ Finger food

Sponsor/Donation/Volunteer Tip(s):

- Find sponsors to offer items to auction or raffle, like a weekend trip to California wine country, bottles of wine, specialty cheeses, or gourmet cookbooks.

- Seek a partnership with a local wine merchant who can offer you his/her expertise and access to a good variety of wine. The merchant will get customers through you and may be able to offer you a price break on the wine. Ask to sell tickets through their store.

- Consider partnering with a small non-profit arts organization such as a chamber music group or jazz ensemble to perform at your event.

- A suitable venue would be a country vineyard or chateau, a garden or other scenic outdoor setting, or an atmospheric inn or lodge is perfect for this event.

Execution Tip(s):

- Have a few volunteers on hand to act as designated drivers for guests who might need a safe lift home.

- Consider having palate cleansing food such as chopped up pieces of cheese, fruit or bread on the table at all times in addition to the paired finger food to go with the wine for guests who would like to clean their palate between each type of wine for a clearer taste.

Games and Contests

Tournament games and contests are a great way to get your community involved while fundraising a fair amount of money but appealing to everyone's competitive side. These events also tend to be family friendly, so a wider population of the community can join in.

Planning

Give yourself at least six months to plan the event, or even up to a year if possible. Planning a major event is similar to planning a big wedding — you need a venue, decorations, entertainment, food and beverages, and a guest list.

Sponsors

Consider asking a business to sponsor the entire event. Know what you can promise them. Offer to include their name or logo on event materials or link to their social media. Remember to further thank your sponsors during the actual event.

Volunteers

Depending on the event you choose, you could need upwards of five volunteers to help judge, referee, participate in, and guide guests during an event. Clean up afterwards may be another task volunteers need to fill since outdoor events can often be messy. However, since these positions need little training and are fairly easy tasks to accomplish, finding volunteers to help out should not be hard.

Venue

The local park, recreation center, or school gym all work for great venues for this type of event. Keep in mind the target number of people you are trying to reach and plan around that number for the venue size. It's better to have a larger venue than needed than for the space to become too crowded.

Preparation

Start off by creating an executive committee that is responsible for major decisions about the auction and delegating work to other committees. Then move on to deciding the type of auction, deciding a venue, sponsors, and fundraising goals. Be confident when asking for donations or sponsorships and be clear in what you are fundraising for; this will make possible sponsors more inclined to help your cause.

From there you can move on to advertising the event to the community using social media, radio commercials, newspaper ads, flyers posted around busy areas of town, and other means. If you can, decide a target audience and cater to these people. It is more effective to directly appeal to a certain audience than trying to encompass the blanket term of 'everyone.' Target audiences can be based on almost anything, but age and location are easy to market to.

Always arrive early to set up the event, and account for time needed to break down and clean up the venue afterwards. For planned activities during the event, consider creating a script for the master of ceremonies to read. Be transparent about the items offered in the event, and do not advertise items that won't be sold or that you cannot guarantee will be sold on auction day. Ideally wait until you have several items and business sponsorships before advertising to the community.

29. Amazing Race

Description: Much like the popular television show, participating teams travel to several checkpoints where they will face challenges before making it to the finish line. The winning team is the team that conquers all of the challenges and arrives at a set location before the other racers. Charge a fee per team to enter the competition. For additional profits, consider requiring an individual pledge donation to your organization.

Estimated Cost:

Levels of Difficulty:

Obtaining Sponsors/Donations	★ ★ ★
Finding a Venue	★ ★ ★
Recruiting Volunteers	★ ★
Preparation	★ ★ ★ ★
Execution	★ ★ ★ ★

Sponsor/Donation/Volunteer Tip(s):

• Have teams gather sponsor donations as they would for a walk-a-thon or other similar events (see the example sponsorship sheet in the back of this book).

• Seek donations for prizes for each member of the winning team.

• You may require multiple venues that your teams will travel to in order to organize a variety of challenges. A large venue like a meeting hall or a school gym will be needed to be a start and finish place.

Execution Tip(s):

- Rules of play should be very specific to avoid discrepancies.

- Have a variety of prizes for categories like "The Silliest Team" or "The Team That Traveled the Farthest."

- Before the event starts, do a walk-through of all the courses to make sure there are no dangerous obstacles or problems with the equipment.

- Have a meet up point at each venue where teams can rest in between each activity while they wait for other teams to finish. Consider having small activities for the teams to do to keep occupied like provide cards and board games as well as refreshments.

30. Cow-Chip Bingo

Description: Find a well-fed cow and a large area, such as a football field, to divide into one-square-yard portions. Sell $30 tickets that give participants a portion of the field as well as a meal. Release the cow and allow it to roam the field until it eliminates. The owner of this section of field wins a prize. Raise additional profits by selling refreshments, holding raffles, and offering prizes. See if a local school will allow you to use a field.

Estimated Cost:

Levels of Difficulty:

Obtaining Sponsors/Donations	⭐⭐⭐
Finding a Venue	⭐⭐
Recruiting Volunteers	⭐⭐
Preparation	⭐⭐⭐
Execution	⭐⭐⭐⭐

Special Materials/Equipment:

- ☐ Well-fed cow

- ☐ Fence

- ☐ Chalk (to grid the field)

Sponsor/Donation/Volunteer Tip(s):

- The best sponsor for this event is a farm or local dairy that will lend its cow.

- Any cow-friendly and spectator-friendly place with a large field is good for a venue.

- Be sure to make clear rules to determine the outcome of the bingo event.

Execution Tip(s):

- Have a volunteer call out bingo spots to the crowd as the cow marks them.

- Considering having a larger grid board easily seen from the audience to also mark claimed bingo spaces on.

Variation Tip(s):

- This is an event that does well combined with another event, such as a field day party or picnic.

- Combining it with other events will draw a larger crowd and help to earn more money.

31. Dart Tournament

Description: For an entry fee, participants can compete in games of darts. Have local restaurants organize teams for the event; reach out to venues that are likely to have darts players, like a bowling alley.

Estimated Cost:

Levels of Difficulty:

Obtaining Sponsors/Donations	✪ ✪
Finding a Venue	✪ ✪ ✪
Recruiting Volunteers	✪ ✪
Preparation	✪ ✪
Execution	✪ ✪

Special Materials/Equipment:

☐ Dartboards

☐ Darts

Sponsor/Donation/Volunteer Tip(s):

- For the venue, a hotel, restaurant, school, church, or any venue equipped for a darts tournament works, especially one that is already set up with dartboards.

- Ask a venue to host your organization for an evening. Generally, you will charge an admission to the venue and require a fee or sponsorship for the teams. If you choose to host this event at a bar, as bars are common location for darts, ensure that you have adults working with you. Discuss with adults whether or not the bar will retain the alcohol sales. You can make other arrangements with the bar, you have to make it attractive to them as well for them to want to host this event. If you plan your event for an evening that is considered an off night for the bar, such as a Monday or Tuesday, and you can guarantee them a full house of your supporters, they will be more than happy to do the event for the sales at the bar.

- In addition to charging an entry fee at the door, have gamers collect pledges and ask for sponsorships (see the sample pledge forms in the back of this book).

- Try to get a local business or restaurant.

Execution Tip(s):

- If your venue is not able to service the whole event itself, enlist volunteers to work hospitality positions and help venue staff.

Variation(s):

- Host a Foosball Tournament.

- Try an Air Hockey Tournament.

- Have a Pinball Tournament.

32. Quiz Show

Description: Smarties will flock to this fun competition to prove their knowledge in a friendly setting.

Estimated Cost:

Levels of Difficulty:

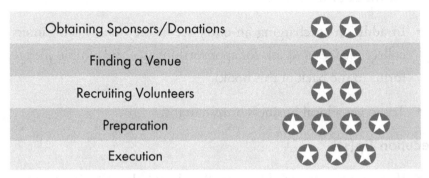

Obtaining Sponsors/Donations	★ ★
Finding a Venue	★ ★
Recruiting Volunteers	★ ★
Preparation	★ ★ ★ ★
Execution	★ ★ ★

Special Materials/Equipment:

☐ List of quiz questions and answers

☐ Stage

☐ Lighting

☐ Sound equipment (microphone, speakers)

☐ Table and chairs

Sponsor/Donation/Volunteer Tip(s):

- Find local businesses to donate their services and items to serve as door prizes for the event.

- An ideal sponsor for such an event is a media sponsor, like a local radio station that could get the word out about the event and provide an MC.

- Ask for participation fees with different set rates for individuals and teams. Consider holding two separate event times for those who want to compete solo and those who want to have a team competition.

- A location with a stage, adequate stage lighting, and an in-house sound system is best for the venue. Consider a local community theater, a banquet hall, or a large meeting room at a hotel.

Execution Tip(s):

- Make sure the rules are clear to avoid discrepancies.

- Double-check the answers to your quiz questions to ensure validity.

33. Scavenger Hunt

Description: Send participating groups on an unforgettable adventure race across town with a list of items and a limited amount of time; charge a sign-up fee to make money for your organization. Everyone can regroup at the end and wait for you to announce the winners. This is a great fundraising event for a church, school, or civic organization.

Estimated Cost:

Levels of Difficulty:

Obtaining Sponsors/Donations	✪ ✪ ✪
Finding a Venue	✪ ✪
Recruiting Volunteers	✪ ✪
Preparation	✪ ✪ ✪ ✪
Execution	✪ ✪ ✪

Sponsor/Donation/Volunteer Tip(s):

- Seek food donors if you plan to serve food at the post-hunt gathering.

- Have teams gather sponsor donations as they would for a walk-a-thon or other similar event. (See the example sponsorship sheet in the back of this book.)

- Seek donations for prizes for the winners. Remember to secure multiple prizes to accommodate all members of the winning team.

- A meeting hall, a school gym, or any place where a large crowd can gather works well for the venue.

- Have volunteers act as checkpoint guides, judges, and announcers for the event.

Execution Tip(s):

- Gather the participants to hand out the scavenger hunt lists and go over the rules.

- Make rules of play clear and specific to avoid discrepancies.

- Start your timer and begin the race.

- As hunters return to the venue, two judges should to mark each team's return time, go over their findings, and determine their scores.

- Have volunteers run game stations and serve food as teams wait for everyone to arrive.

- At the appointed hour, announce the winners and award prizes.

- Have a variety of prizes for things like "The Silliest Team," "The Team That Traveled the Farthest," or "The Youngest/Oldest Team." It is always fun to have many winners.

34. Scrabble Tournament

Description: Participants can have a blast playing with words at a fundraising scrabble tournament. Teams of four, six, or eight will be provided a scrabble board and letters. Start each group with the same word and give them 20 minutes to fill the board up with their own words. A judge will be present at every table, and players who need extra help can donate money to glance at a dictionary. Charge an entry fee for each player in the tournament. Sell concessions or hold a raffle to make extra profits.

Estimated Cost:

Levels of Difficulty:

Obtaining Sponsors/Donations	⭐⭐
Finding a Venue	⭐⭐
Recruiting Volunteers	⭐⭐
Preparation	⭐⭐
Execution	⭐⭐

Special Materials/Equipment:

☐ Scrabble games

☐ Tables and chairs

Sponsor/Donation/Volunteer Tip(s):

- A toy store, game store, or large department store that sells games might be a good sponsor for this event. Ideally, you can get your games donated.

- Find a venue to host the event. For a place like a pub, generally, you will collect an admission fee and a sponsorship fee for gamers, and the pub will take the alcohol sales. If you plan your event for a night that is considered an "off night" for the facility, such as a Monday or Tuesday, and you can guarantee them a full house of your supporters, they will likely be glad to do the event for the sales at the bar.

- You can also have gamers collect pledges (see the sample pledge forms in the back of this book).

- You can make game boards yourself if money is tight.

Execution Tip(s):

- Have volunteers act as judges and referees for the individual games to ensure smooth playing.

Variation(s):

- Hold a Monopoly, Boggle, or Uno Tournament.

35. Snow/Sand Sculptures

Description: Fancy snow or sand sculptures always catch the eyes of passersby. Find an expert sculptor who can create something attention-grabbing in a highly-trafficked public place. People will be eager to meet the individual and learn a few tips on his or her skill. Allow teams or individuals to participate and set an entrance fee.

Estimated Cost:

Levels of Difficulty:

Obtaining Sponsors/Donations	✪ ✪ ✪
Finding a Venue	✪ ✪ ✪
Recruiting Volunteers	✪ ✪
Preparation	✪ ✪ ✪
Execution	✪ ✪

Special Materials/Equipment:

☐ Sand or snow

☐ Shovels and other sculpting tools

Sponsors/Donations:

• Your organization can seek sculptors to offer their time and services for a sculpting workshop.

- The beach is a great venue for sand sculptures, and a large parking lot works well for snow sculptures. A park is a fine place for smaller sculptures.

- If you are in a snowy climate and are considering doing large-scale snow sculptures, talk to the local authorities about bringing snow cleared from city streets to your location for the event. By providing this much extra snow, you can promote the possibility of building humongous sculptures.

Execution Tip(s):

- Give a designated time for when all sculptures should be done and ready for viewing.

- Have volunteers patrol the space to make sure the artists are given proper room from the attendees to work and to make sure no accidents happen.

Variation(s):

- Turn the event into a summer/winter carnival by adding games and other activities you can charge people to participate in.

- Hold a silent auction or raffle at your event to increase your ability to raise funds. A good auction/raffle item for a snow-sculpting event is a vacation to a warm and sunny climate.

Holidays and Special Occasions

Many holidays are supposed to be celebrated with others so putting together a fundraising event to cater towards the community is a perfect way to appeal to the charity in others while commemorating the holiday.

Planning

Give yourself at least six months to plan the event, or even up to a year if possible. Planning a major event is similar to planning a big wedding — you need a venue, decorations, entertainment, food and beverages, and a guest list.

Sponsors

Consider asking a business to sponsor the entire event. Know what you can promise them. Offer to include their name or logo on event materials or link to their social media. Remember to further thank your sponsors during the actual event.

Volunteers

Depending upon the kind of holiday event you host, 10-15 volunteers should be sufficient to handle guests, serving food if needed, and making any necessary announcements throughout the night.

Venue

Hotels with large ballrooms, country clubs, school auditoriums or gyms are natural places to properly host these kinds of events.

Preparation

Start off by creating an executive committee that is responsible for major decisions about the auction and delegating work to other committees. Then move on to deciding the type of auction, deciding a venue, sponsors, and fundraising goals. Be confident when asking for donations or sponsorships, and be clear about what you are fundraising for; this will make possible sponsors more inclined to help your cause.

From there you can move on to advertising the event to the community using social media, radio commercials, newspaper ads, flyers posted around busy areas of town, and other means. If you can, decide a target audience and cater to these people. It is more effective to directly appeal to a certain audience than trying to encompass the blanket term of 'everyone.' Target audiences can be based on almost anything, but age and location are easy to market to.

Always arrive early to set up for the event, and account for time needed to break down and clean up afterwards. For planned activities during the event, consider creating a script for the master of ceremonies to read. Be transparent about the items offered in the event, and do not advertise items that won't be sold or that you cannot guarantee will be sold on auction day. Ideally wait until you have several items and business sponsorships before advertising to the community.

36. Birthday Banquet

Description: Your organization can offer to throw a birthday bash for a regular supporter or donor. Set the theme for the event around the person's favorite hobby, movie, or other interest. Charge a fee to cover general admission and dinner expenses. Food and drinks can also focus on the theme chosen by the birthday honoree. Consider hosting it for a prominent individual in your school, or a faculty member that sponsors your club.

Estimated Cost:

Levels of Difficulty:

Obtaining Sponsors/Donations	⭐⭐
Finding a Venue	⭐⭐
Recruiting Volunteers	⭐⭐
Preparation	⭐⭐⭐
Execution	⭐⭐⭐

Special Materials/Equipment:

☐ Banquet tables

☐ Chairs

☐ Sound equipment (microphone, speakers)

☐ Specialty lighting

Sponsor/Donation/Volunteer Tip(s):

• The best donation that you could get is a venue.

- Consider having local restaurants or grocery stores donate food and the birthday cake to fit the theme of the night.

- If you are having this as a school fundraiser, consider having the event in the school gymnasium. If the event is for your church, and you can the event in the social hall in your building. If you want to go all out for this event, consider having it at an upscale hotel in your community or any venue with a fancy banquet room.

Execution Tip(s):

- Have volunteers act as the wait staff and serve food.

Variation(s):

- Celebrate the anniversary of a company, a big accomplishment, or a couple at an Anniversary Banquet.

- Gather people and their furry friends for a Pet Birthday Banquet.

37. Halloween Costume Party

Description: Celebrate Halloween with a fun and extravagant costume party. Charge an admission fee.

Estimated Cost:

Levels of Difficulty:

Obtaining Sponsors/Donations	⭐⭐⭐
Finding a Venue	⭐⭐⭐⭐
Recruiting Volunteers	⭐⭐
Preparation	⭐⭐⭐⭐
Execution	⭐⭐⭐⭐

Special Materials/Equipment:

☐ Black and orange decorations

☐ Dance floor

☐ Sound system

☐ Music

Sponsor/Donation/Volunteer Tip(s):

- Local theaters and performing arts organizations are great places to seek donations of costumes and props for this event.

- Theatrical prop companies are also good places to locate supplies for the event.

- Nice hotels are great places for such parties because they can usually handle the catering and provide an in-house sound system, lighting, and large ballrooms that can accommodate many people. Unusual locations like large old houses, churches, or inns are also fitting.

Execution Tip(s):

- Hold a costume contest at the banquet, and give prizes for the Best Handmade or Most Creative costumes, etc.

- Play a horror/slasher movie to further set the mood. Dracula and Halloween are classic choices, and Texas Chainsaw Massacre and Saw will amp up the gore. The Addams Family, The Nightmare Before Christmas, or Halloweentown are more child-friendly choices.

38. Christmas Tree Sale

Description: Set up a colorfully lit, festive lot and offer a variety of healthy trees and wreaths for sale. Profit from these big purchases and the tips that come from cutting the trees and loading them into customers' vehicles. Play Christmas music to get everyone in the holiday spirit and sell Christmas cookies and hot chocolate for extra profit.

Estimated Cost:

Levels of Difficulty:

Obtaining Sponsors/Donations	⭐⭐⭐⭐
Finding a Venue	⭐⭐⭐
Recruiting Volunteers	⭐⭐⭐⭐
Preparation	⭐⭐⭐⭐⭐
Execution	⭐⭐⭐⭐⭐

Special Materials/Equipment:

☐ Tent

☐ Christmas trees

☐ Tree stands

☐ Netting, rope, razor, etc. (to package trees)

☐ Chainsaw (to cut bases of trees)

☐ Outdoor lighting

☐ Giant sign (to make it easy to read from the road)

☐ Christmas lights

☐ Christmas music

Sponsor/Donation/Volunteer Tip(s):

- Try to find tree farmers who are willing to donate trees or sell them at a reduced price to support your cause.

- Ask stores that sell tree stands if they will donate stands or sell them at a reduced price.

- A supermarket parking lot, your organization's lot, or places bordering a main road are great venues to catch drivers who are on the hunt for a tree.

- Have volunteers help customers select a tree, cut it down, and move it to their car.

- Take advantage of your school's network and ask your friends' and their parents to purchase their trees from you.

Execution Tip(s):

- Put lights on your sign to ensure that your lot is visible to shoppers at night.

- Advertise free hot chocolate to get more people to stop by.

- Sell hand-made ornaments for additional profit.

Variation(s):

- Offer a service to pick up old Christmas trees for a fee or donation. Advertise with fliers at tree lots, shopping centers, and neighborhoods throughout December and early January.

39. "Hats Off to Mom" Tea Party

Description: Mothers and daughters will enjoy a delightful afternoon wearing hats and gloves, eating finger sandwiches, and sipping tea from fancy tea sets. Put a box of fun craft supplies on each table, and have guests make their own hats to model at the end. Set up a photo booth and sell mother-daughter photos to guests.

Estimated Cost: $ $ $ $

Levels of Difficulty:

Obtaining Sponsors/Donations	★★★
Finding a Venue	★★
Recruiting Volunteers	★★
Preparation	★★★★
Execution	★★★★

Special Materials/Equipment:

- [ ] Basic straw hats

- [ ] Hat decorations (scarves, ribbons, feathers, fake flowers, tissue paper, streamers)

- [ ] Tea and tea sets

- [ ] Banquet tables and chairs

- [ ] Sound system (microphone, speakers)

Sponsor/Donation/Volunteer Tip(s):

- If there is a hat shop in your community, they could be your best sponsor.

- Find a venue willing to lend their facility for free; perhaps a nice hotel, restaurant, or country club.

- Contact local craft stores for donations of decorations.

- Consider partnering with a small nonprofit arts organization such as a chamber music group or jazz ensemble to perform at your event.

Execution Tip(s):

- Schedule this event around Mother's Day.

Variation(s):

- Have a Mother-Daughter Spa Day.

- Have a Father-Son event, like a sailing, golfing, or fishing tournament.

40. Holiday Card Mailings

Description: While everyone is in the spirit of giving, wish them happy holidays and make it easy for them to give your organization a gift in return. Enclose a donation card and no-postage-necessary envelopes. Send them early so you are one of the first to ask for donations.

Estimated Cost:

Levels of Difficulty:

Obtaining Sponsors/Donations	⭐⭐
Finding a Venue	N/A
Recruiting Volunteers	⭐⭐
Preparation	⭐⭐
Execution	⭐⭐

Special Materials/Equipment:

- ☐ Card paper

- ☐ Envelopes

- ☐ No-postage-necessary return envelops

- ☐ Address labels (unless you plan to print the information directly on the envelop)

Sponsor/Donation/Volunteer Tip(s):

- A local hobby or craft store is the ideal sponsor for such an event.

- Any empty large space that can get a little messy and can have tables and chairs set up will work as the venue.

Execution Tip(s):

- To maximize efficiency, form assembly lines in which one person puts the address labels on the envelope, one stuffs the envelope, and one seals it.

- You can do this event for any kind of holiday or event that people send cards on, but the big payday will come as you approach Christmas.

- Do this annually and build a mailing list that grows each year.

Variation(s):

- Instead of sending the traditional, store-bought cards, you can make yours stand out by making them. You could have an event or two leading up to the mailing where families, groups, etc. are invited to craft cards with the aid of instructors. Ask volunteers to bring their own scissors, glue, and other craft supplies, if needed, to make the process quicker and easier.

41. Holiday Carnival

Description: Celebrate the holidays with festive decorations and music as well as themed food and games. The possibilities are endless.

Estimated Cost:

Levels of Difficulty:

Obtaining Sponsors/Donations	★★★
Finding a Venue	★★
Recruiting Volunteers	★★★★
Preparation	★★★★
Execution	★★★★

Special Materials/Equipment:

☐ Holiday decorations

☐ Holiday food

☐ Holiday game/activity equipment

☐ Sound system (microphone, speakers)

Sponsor/Donation/Volunteer Tip(s):

• Find people to donate food, games, and crafts that will be used to generate holiday spirit and revenue.

• This is best held at your organization's base, whether this be a church, school, or community center.

- Enlist volunteers to handle the food, greetings, announcements, and other planned events and games at the party.

Execution Tip(s):

- Weekend afternoons work best for this event.

- Have a variety of games and activities for people to participate in. Consider playing music and leaving a space open for dancing as well.

Variation(s):

- Cater the theme to the time of year. For example, celebrate the changing colors of leaves and crisp fall air by holding a fall fiesta. Feature a buffet-style dinner and auction fall food favorites, like honey ham, turkey, or pumpkin pie. Offer activities such as pumpkin carving, pumpkin painting, and scarecrow making, and offer prizes in different categories (most creative, silliest, etc.). If you hold the event in the park, consider equipment and materials for field activities such as a hayride, corn maze, or game of gourd toss.

42. Kentucky Derby Party

Description: Host a watch party the day of the Kentucky Derby race. Encourage attendants to dress up and wear their best fancy hats to the party. Charge an admission fee or have attendants bid on who they think will win the race, with the knowledge that their bids will go towards the fundraiser.

Estimated Cost:

Levels of Difficulty:

Obtaining Sponsors/Donations	★ ★ ★
Finding a Venue	★ ★
Recruiting Volunteers	★ ★
Preparation	★ ★ ★
Execution	★ ★

Sponsor/Donation/Volunteer Tip(s):

- Find a bar, restaurant, or hotel with access to a television and room fit for a large audience that would allow you to show the Kentucky Derby during the party. Try to get catering from the same place. You can also just host the event at your organization base if you have a television and have a local restaurant cater instead.

- Get sponsors or donations from other businesses to buy nice decorations to cover the event. Offer to advertise their business during the party and through the promotion of the event on social media and elsewhere.

- Have volunteers help as service staff to make sure food and drink are properly restocked when needed.

Execution Tip(s):

- Host a hat contest during the party with a prize such as a gift card to a popular local boutique to gain more interest. Have the boutique donate the gift card with the promise of promotion and encourage attendees to go there to shop.

- Have a gratitude prize either for whoever bids the most money or for who bid the most money on the winning horse.

43. Mardi Gras Party

Description: This celebration will offer participants a chance to eat, drink, and be merry while dressed in outrageous costumes and beaded necklaces. Be sure to serve delectable New Orleans-style food and feature a live jazz band for the event. With this theme, you can incorporate many different fundraisers, such as raffles, wine tasting, gourmet food, and auctions.

Estimated Cost:

Levels of Difficulty:

Obtaining Sponsors/Donations	✪ ✪ ✪
Finding a Venue	✪
Recruiting Volunteers	✪ ✪ ✪
Preparation	✪ ✪ ✪
Execution	✪ ✪ ✪ ✪

Special Materials/Equipment:

☐ Mardi Gras decorations

☐ Masks

☐ Beads

☐ Party favors

Sponsor/Donation/Volunteer Tip(s):

- Ask Cajun and New Orleans-style restaurants to donate food. These can also be a possible option for a venue if the restaurant is willing since it will cut out the need for decorations.

- Request donations of crafts supplies for decorations from craft stores. Or, if there is a party store in the area, ask them to donate Mardi Gras themed decorations.

- Possible venue places include your organization's base or a nice hotel ballroom.

Execution Tip(s):

- Play a variety of Cajun music and jazz for the attendants to dance to. Consider having a local band who plays the right style of music donating some of their time to play during the event.

- If you choose to host any sort of auction, raffle, or other fund-raising event during the night, disperse the event throughout the night so attendees don't feel bombarded with you asking for money and are more likely to spend money again on items.

Variation(s):

- Throw a St. Patrick's Day Party

- Hold a Valentine's Day Party

- Host an Independence Day Festival

44. Oscar Party

Description: Encourage participants to dress in elegant attire fit for a star and walk the red carpet as they arrive at your Oscar-inspired banquet. Charge a fee for admission to the event and provide a catered dinner with gourmet food. Present an award for the best dressed at the event.

Estimated Cost:

Levels of Difficulty:

Obtaining Sponsors/Donations	⭐⭐
Finding a Venue	⭐⭐
Recruiting Volunteers	⭐⭐
Preparation	⭐⭐⭐
Execution	⭐⭐⭐

Special Materials/Equipment:

☐ Banquet tables

☐ Chairs

☐ Sound equipment (microphone, speakers)

☐ Specialty lighting

☐ Red carpet

Sponsor/Donation/Volunteer Tip(s):

• The best donation that you might possibly get is that of a venue.

- Try to find someone to sponsor the entire event or see if you can get sponsors for each banquet table.

- Consider having it at an upscale hotel in your community or any venue with a fancy banquet room.

Execution Tip(s):

- Hold this event on the night of the Oscars for a fun, classy viewing party.

- Remember that you cannot use the words "Oscar" or "Academy Award" in your marketing unless you obtain permission to do so, but you can strongly hint by saying things like "the biggest night in Hollywood" or "star-studded awards show."

45. Parent Appreciation Banquet

Description: Teens will have the opportunity to express their love and gratitude for their parents in this fundraising event. Gather several students from local schools to send out invitations to their parents and charge a fee for attendance. The teens will act as the servers at the banquet. Play interactive games with all the guests involved.

Estimated Cost:

Levels of Difficulty:

Obtaining Sponsors/Donations	⭐ ⭐
Finding a Venue	⭐ ⭐
Recruiting Volunteers	⭐ ⭐
Preparation	⭐ ⭐ ⭐
Execution	⭐ ⭐ ⭐

Special Materials/Equipment:

- ☐ Banquet tables

- ☐ Chairs

- ☐ Sound equipment (microphone, speakers)

- ☐ Specialty lighting

Sponsor/Donation/Volunteer Tip(s):

- If you are doing this fundraiser for your school Parent-Teacher Organization, consider having the event in the gymnasium of the school. If the event is for your church and you have a social hall in your building, have the event there. If you want to go all out, consider having it at an upscale hotel in your community or any venue with a fancy banquet room.

Execution Tip(s):

- Have a special presentation from a guest speaker.

- Have kids make cards, crafts, or placemats to put at their parents' seat or to give to them at a designated time.

Variation(s):

- Have a Kid Appreciation Banquet.

- Put on a Spouse Appreciation Banquet.

- Hold a Teacher Appreciation Banquet.

46. Pumpkin Fest

Description: Have a pumpkin-filled festival featuring a pumpkin pie bake-off, pumpkin juice, pumpkin carving and painting stations, and pumpkin games for people of all ages. Charge a fee for admission.

Estimated Cost:

Levels of Difficulty:

Obtaining Sponsors/Donations	★ ★ ★
Finding a Venue	★ ★
Recruiting Volunteers	★ ★
Preparation	★ ★ ★
Execution	★ ★ ★

Special Materials/Equipment:

☐ Pumpkins

☐ Paint

☐ Brushes

☐ Carving knives

☐ Serving utensils (for the pies)

☐ Pumpkin juice

☐ Pumpkin game supplies

Sponsor/Donation/Volunteer Tip(s):

- Ask pumpkin patches and grocery stores to donate or give you a discount on pumpkins and carving supplies.

- Ask a craft store to donate paints and brushes.

- If you are doing an outdoor festival, secure a park pavilion. You can also consider holding the event in your organization's parking lot, especially if your organization is a church or school with heavy foot traffic.

Execution Tip(s):

- Consider also having contests and prizes for the best pumpkin pie or best carved pumpkin to inspire community participation. Find local businesses that are willing to donate gift cards or other prizes.

47. "Soup"er Bowl Sale

Description: Sell hand-painted soup bowls for Super Bowl Sunday. Have artistic volunteers paint soup bowls with the Super Bowl logo, competing teams' colors, or general football theme. Have the bowls fired in a kiln and sell them with a recipe for or a dried package of starter contents for a delicious chili, stew, or other soup that could be made for Super Bowl Sunday. This is a great project for an art school or an organization with ties to artists.

Estimated Cost:

Levels of Difficulty:

Obtaining Sponsors/Donations	★★★
Finding a Venue	★★★★
Recruiting Volunteers	★★★
Preparation	★★★★★
Execution	★★★★

Special Materials/Equipment:

- ☐ Bowls

- ☐ Paint and brushes

- ☐ Kiln

Sponsor/Donation/Volunteer Tip(s):

- Ask local art, craft, or ceramic pottery store for donations of bowls and paints.

- Partner with a ceramics studio or an art school for help painting and seek permission to use their kiln.

- See if a soup company will donate the dried soup mixes and recipes to put with the bowls.

- A church social hall, school cafeteria, or any place with room for large tables to work at is fine for painting. Find a ceramic pottery studio that has a kiln you can use to fire the bowls. Sell bowls through your website and by setting up tables outside of sports bars and at your organization's facility the month leading up to the Super Bowl.

Execution Tip(s):

- Advertise them as great bowls for serving other snacks like chips, dip, salsa, guacamole, candy, or popcorn at your Super Bowl party.

- Make sure the materials used will make a final product that is safe to eat out of.

Variation(s):

- Sell tickets for a soup lunch where you get to take home the hand-painted bowl you ate out of.

- Buy pre-made bowls that are in team colors and sell them with soup-mix or recipes.

- Sell painted holiday cookie jars filled with cookies or cookie-making ingredients inside.

48. White Wonderland Gift Exchange

Description: Let it snow with gifts and donations. During the holidays, catch guests in the spirit of giving by asking them to bring snow-white gifts wrapped in white paper and ribbon to a gift exchange. Set up a donation table and encourage guests to bring a gift to trade and a gift to donate, or to make monetary donations to your organization.

Estimated Cost:

Levels of Difficulty:

Obtaining Sponsors/Donations	⭐⭐⭐
Finding a Venue	⭐
Recruiting Volunteers	⭐⭐⭐
Preparation	⭐⭐⭐⭐
Execution	⭐⭐⭐⭐

Special Materials/Equipment:

- ☐ Festive, white decorations
- ☐ Banquet tables
- ☐ Chairs
- ☐ Specialty lighting
- ☐ Sound equipment (microphone, speakers)

Sponsor/Donation/Volunteer Tip(s):

- Ask local supermarkets and restaurants to donate food or cater the event.

- If you plan for a large event, consider doing your party at a nice hotel with banquet facilities. For a smaller party, consider doing it at someone's home.

Execution Tip(s):

- Paper snowflakes are inexpensive, easy-to-make winter decorations.

- Consider making a wish list for people to look at to give ideas of what to gift.

Variation(s):

- Rent a snow machine. While parents do a gift exchange and socialize, they can pay for their kids to play in the snow and enter a snowman-building contest. The winner will get a prize.

- Giftwrap people's gifts for donations.

Shows

Shows can be a great way to appeal to your community and fundraise because they often offer a spectacle or something interesting for the community to be involved in or watch. Events, such as talent shows, also offer a chance for your community to be directly involved with the fundraising process even if they can't necessarily donate money.

Planning

Give yourself at least six months to plan the event, or even up to a year if possible. Planning a major event is like planning a big wedding — you need a venue, decorations, entertainment, food and beverages, and a guest list.

Sponsors

Consider asking a business to sponsor the entire event. Know what you can promise them. Offer to include their name or logo on event materials or link to their social media. Remember to further thank your sponsors during the actual event.

Volunteers

Depending upon what kind of show you put on, 10-15 volunteers should be sufficient to greet and guide guests, provide informal security, and help planned activities run smoothly.

Venue

Hotels with large ballrooms, country clubs, school auditoriums or gyms are natural places to properly host these kinds of events.

Preparation

Start off by creating an executive committee that is responsible for major decisions about the show and delegating work to other committees. Then move on to deciding the type of show, deciding a venue, sponsors, and fundraising goals. Be confident when asking for donations or sponsorships and be clear in what you are fundraising for; this will make possible sponsors more inclined to help your cause. From there you can move on to advertising the event to the community using social media, radio commercials, newspaper ads, flyers posted around busy areas of town, and other means. If you can, decide a target audience and cater to these people. It is more effective to directly appeal to a certain audience than trying to encompass the blanket term of 'everyone.' Target audiences can be based on almost anything, but age and location are easy to market to. Always arrive early to set up the event, and account for time needed to break down and clean up the venue afterwards. For planned activities during the event, consider creating a script for the master of ceremonies to read. Be transparent about the items offered in the event, and do not advertise items that won't be sold or that you cannot guarantee will be sold on auction day. Ideally wait until you have several items and business sponsorships before advertising to the community.

49. Antique Show

Description: Contact numerous antique dealers in your area and charge each for their own space in the show. Come up with an admission fee and provide food and beverages at the event. Make program books and distribute them to participants.

Estimated Cost:

Levels of Difficulty:

Obtaining Sponsors/Donations	⭐⭐⭐
Finding a Venue	⭐⭐⭐
Recruiting Volunteers	⭐⭐
Preparation	⭐⭐⭐
Execution	⭐⭐⭐

Special Materials/Equipment:

☐ Booths or tables (to showcase antiques)

Sponsor/Donation/Volunteer Tip(s):

- Seek a corporate or business sponsor, like a high-end antique dealer, to cover the venue cost and/or the cost of display materials.

- If you are going to be showing high-end antiques, be sure that you offer the collectors and dealers a secure venue.

- Have volunteers help supervise the show floor to make sure no foul play is committed and to direct guests to where certain collections of antiques may be.

Execution Tip(s):

- Attract dealers and collectors by offering to pass along any mailing lists you generate from this event.

- Meet with the dealers and collectors individually to work out any marketing hooks that will help you to advertise your event and their items.

- Consider offering the antique show along with dinner and/or cocktails. Consider having a wide selection of antiques for show and for sale. Offer a little something for everyone to increase the appeal of the show and increase the likelihood that the dealers will find new customers.

- Categorize the displayed antiques into sections so people searching for particular antiques can find what they want easily.

50. Art Show

Description: Everyone can appreciate quality art and feel good about supporting local artists. Sell tickets for an art gala at which the public can meet with the artists as well as bid for artwork during an auction.

Estimated Cost:

Levels of Difficulty:

Obtaining Sponsors/Donations	⭐ ⭐ ⭐ ⭐
Finding a Venue	⭐ ⭐ ⭐
Recruiting Volunteers	⭐ ⭐
Preparation	⭐ ⭐ ⭐
Execution	⭐ ⭐ ⭐

Special Materials/Equipment:

☐ Supplies for displaying the art

Sponsor/Donation/Volunteer Tip(s):

- Find a corporate or business sponsor to cover the venue cost and/or the cost of display materials. Art supply stores are good places to go.

- Find a caterer or people to cook and/or donate food.

Execution Tip(s):

- To add to the funds you raise, have artists pay a fee for their booths.

- To ensure this is a win-win event for your organization and the artists, make sure you offer to pass along any mailing list you generate from this event to the artists. Also, meet with the artists individually to work out any marketing hooks that will help you to advertise your event and help them promote their works.

- If you are showing high-end art, ensure the safety of artists' work by choosing a secure venue, possibly with security guards.

- Consider having a wide selection of art and pricing structures so there is something for everyone; this will increase the appeal of the show and increase the likelihood that the art will sell.

- Have invitations and tickets designed by an artist and printed on high-quality paper. Make the invitations extra artsy by printing them on CDs, wine glasses, or paper bags.

Variation(s):

- Have a private showing period prior to the event's advertised start time. Sell these tickets separate for a higher price for early admittance to view the art and speak with the artists.

- Introduce your art show fundraiser by hosting a paid preview with dinner.

51. Car Show

Description: Rev up funds with a classic car show. Have local car dealers exhibit cars and charge an admission fee for spectators.

Estimated Cost:

Levels of Difficulty:

Obtaining Sponsors/Donations	✪✪✪
Finding a Venue	✪✪
Recruiting Volunteers	✪✪
Preparation	✪✪✪
Execution	✪✪✪

Special Materials/Equipment:

☐ Classic cars

Sponsor/Donation/Volunteer Tip(s):

- The best sponsors you can have for such an event are the classic cars clubs. You can find a car club in your area on Hubcapcafe's website at **www.hubcapcafe.com.**

- New car dealers can be valuable sponsors for such events.

- If your organization has a large parking lot, that is probably the best venue. If you do not have a parking lot, or if you have a small parking lot, consider a city park's lot, a mall parking lot, or a new car dealership's parking lot.

Execution Tip(s):

- Have a designed pamphlet to give admitted guests with each car exhibited which includes information like the make, model, year, and other important or interesting details about the cars on display.

Variation(s):

- Have a Motorcycle Show.

- A great indoor event is a Classic (Antique) Toy Show.

52. Comedy Club Night

Description: Have a laugh-out-load evening and smile about your profits. Sell tickets for an evening at a comedy club.

Estimated Cost:

Levels of Difficulty:

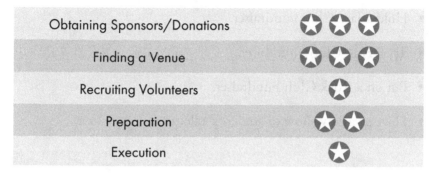

Obtaining Sponsors/Donations	★ ★ ★
Finding a Venue	★ ★ ★
Recruiting Volunteers	★
Preparation	★ ★
Execution	★

Sponsor/Donation/Volunteer Tip(s):

- Ask a local comedy club to host this event for an evening and have the proceeds donated to your organization. The comedy club will schedule the comedians.

- Besides holding this event at a comedy club, consider having it at a restaurant, school, church, or any venue with a stage.

Execution Tip(s):

- Remember to publicly thank the club during the event.

- Generally, you will take the sales of the admission to the club and the club will take the sales at the bar. You can make other arrangements with the club, but you have to make it attractive to them. If you plan your event for a night that is considered an "off night" for the club, such as a Monday or Tuesday, and you can guarantee them a full house of your supporters, they will be more than happy to do the event for the sales at the bar.

- Students and members of your organization can perform the acts for the night.

Variation(s):

- Hold a Jazz Club Fundraiser.

- Try a Folk Club Fundraiser.

- Put on a Rock Club Fundraiser.

- Have a variety show of students' talents.

53. Concert in the Park

Description: Holding a concert in the park can be a huge fundraising success. Local talents will be eager to showcase their skills, and they will likely play for free to gain recognition in the community. This event is ideal for children and teen volunteers.

Estimated Cost:

Levels of Difficulty:

Obtaining Sponsors/Donations	✪ ✪ ✪
Finding a Venue	✪ ✪ ✪
Recruiting Volunteers	✪ ✪
Preparation	✪ ✪ ✪ ✪
Execution	✪ ✪ ✪ ✪

Special Materials/Equipment:

☐ Sound equipment (microphone, speakers)

☐ Stage

☐ Seating

Sponsor/Donation/Volunteer Tip(s):

- Contact local businesses to act as event sponsors. Set sponsorship levels and offer potential sponsors advertising rights, select seating, and other perks to make sponsorship attractive.

- Try to find well-known musicians who support your cause to perform.

- A park with a band shell, outdoor amphitheater, or hill to serve as a natural amphitheater work well as venues.

Execution Tip(s):

- To save the money and hassle of renting and setting up chairs, advertise, "Bring a blanket and sit on the lawn under the stars." If you choose to have the concert near a hill, have people sit toward the top of the hill with a good view of the performers at the bottom of the hill.

- Coordinate with your school's music programs and split the donations with them. Use your organization's network and financial support for hosting the event as an incentive.

54. Fashion Show

Description: Have models or confident volunteers strut their stuff while excited audience members gain insight into the latest styles and newest trends. A fashion show is a great way to gain immense profits for your organization.

Estimated Cost:

Levels of Difficulty:

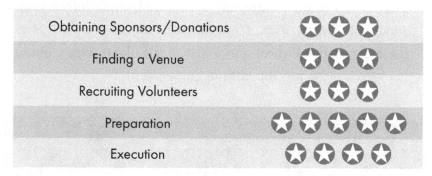

Obtaining Sponsors/Donations	★ ★ ★
Finding a Venue	★ ★ ★
Recruiting Volunteers	★ ★ ★
Preparation	★ ★ ★ ★ ★
Execution	★ ★ ★ ★

Special Materials/Equipment:

☐ Stage

☐ Catwalk

☐ Sound equipment (microphone, speakers)

Sponsor/Donation/Volunteer Tip(s):

- Ask a few larger stores at a mall or some smaller boutiques to show their seasonal fashions for a sponsorship fee of $30 to $50 per item shown or ask for a sponsorship donation of $500 to $1,000.

- A country club restaurant or a local hotel is an excellent venue if you are serving a meal at your event. If you are just serving hors d'oeuvres and beverages, consider a local community theater, which will provide you with a stage, sound equipment, and lighting.

Execution Tip(s):

- To generate more profit, have volunteer photographers document each look that is showcased, and create a photo book with descriptions of each outfit and sponsors. Include information about your organization. Contact attendees about a week after the event to thank them and ask if they'd like to buy a photo book for a memento and fashion guide or gift.

Variation(s):

- Plan an outdoor fashion event such as a garden party.

- Choose to have the modeled items be designed by students.

- Have experimental fashions that might be considered works of art.

- Feature hairstyles.

- Do a fashion show for children.

- Have members of your organization design outfits.

55. Home and Garden Show

Description: Attendees will be excited to beautify their yards by making purchases for their new paradises. At a large meeting center, feature a variety of garden items available for purchase by selling booth space to gardening vendors, nurseries, gazebo suppliers, and others who sell products relating to outdoor home living.

Estimated Cost:

Levels of Difficulty:

Obtaining Sponsors/Donations	✪ ✪ ✪ ✪
Finding a Venue	✪ ✪ ✪ ✪
Recruiting Volunteers	✪ ✪ ✪
Preparation	✪ ✪ ✪ ✪
Execution	✪ ✪ ✪ ✪

Special Materials/Equipment:

☐ Booths, lighting and sound equipment (if not provided by the venue)

Sponsor/Donation/Volunteer Tip(s):

• Large local nurseries are ideal sponsors for such events, as are hardware, home, and garden retailers.

• Seek early partnerships with local merchants who will attract people to your event by providing on-site expertise in home and gardening matters.

- Consider partnering with a bluegrass band to perform at your event.

- Book a large meeting center, such as a convention center, that can have indoor and outdoor display space as your venue.

Execution Tip(s):

- Have volunteers help move sold plants from the show area to the cars of the buyers. Have a designated pick up station where volunteers move plants to where the buyers can drive up, double-check the order, and then load the plants into their cars.

56. Horse Show

Description: Charge participants to compete in a horse show. Provide cash prizes for first, second, and third place. Charge an admission fee for the audience and sell concessions and chances at winning door prizes.

Estimated Cost:

Levels of Difficulty:

Obtaining Sponsors/Donations	⭐⭐⭐
Finding a Venue	⭐⭐⭐
Recruiting Volunteers	⭐⭐
Preparation	⭐⭐⭐⭐
Execution	⭐⭐⭐⭐

Sponsor/Donation/Volunteer Tip(s):

- A stable, barn, or riding school may be an excellent sponsor. Consider asking them to serve as the venue as well.

- Companies that make and/or sell riding equipment may also be good sponsors and prize donors.

Execution Tip(s):

- Have volunteer photographers document the event and offer to sell photo books or framed photographs to participants after the show.

- Have a children's ride available where parents can pay a small fee for their children to ride a pony.

57. Host a Radio Show

Description: Go live on the air and host a talk show promoting your cause. Feature guests who are knowledgeable about your cause or who have first-hand experience. This is a good fundraiser because people can call in and/or send donations and you can have conversations with listeners interested in your organization.

Estimated Cost:

Levels of Difficulty:

Obtaining Sponsors/Donations	⭐⭐⭐
Finding a Venue	⭐⭐
Recruiting Volunteers	⭐
Preparation	⭐⭐
Execution	⭐⭐

Sponsors/Donations:

• The best sponsor you can have for such an event is a popular radio station that also doubles as the venue.

Execution Tip(s):

• Arrive with your notes and supporters who will give testimonials.

• Go live on the air and convince listeners to donate.

• Prepare your statement of need so as not to ask for a handout but, rather, as an invitation to people to work in partnership with you toward your organizational goals.

58. Karaoke Celebration

Description: Profits from this entertaining evening will be music to your ears as old and new performers alike pay to be in the spotlight for a few songs. Supply contestants with funny, original costumes and props. Participants pay an entry fee and are provided with a song list and pledge sheet before the event takes place. Friends can support karaoke contestants by pledging an amount of their choice. Audience members can also pay to stop performers from singing.

Estimated Cost:

Levels of Difficulty:

Obtaining Sponsors/Donations	⭐⭐
Finding a Venue	⭐⭐⭐
Recruiting Volunteers	⭐⭐
Preparation	⭐⭐
Execution	⭐⭐

Special Materials/Equipment:

☐ Karaoke machine

Sponsor/Donation/Volunteer Tip(s):

- Contact a local karaoke club and ask if it will donate its club to your organization for an evening. Generally, you will take the sales of the admission to the club and the club will take the sales at the bar. You can make other arrangements with the club, but you have to make it attractive to them, as well. If you plan your event for a night that is considered an "off night" for the club, such as a Monday or Tuesday, and you can guarantee them a full house of your supporters, they will be more than happy to do the event for the sales at the club.

- Ask organization members to lend costumes and props for performers to borrow.

Execution Tip(s):

- Remember to publicly thank the club during the event.

- If you choose to hold your event at a location other than a karaoke club, you can either rent a karaoke machine or hire a DJ to come in and MC the event. The easiest thing to do is to hire a DJ. This may add to your costs, but it will make the event a little easier for you to put together. When you interview DJs to do this type of event, ask how big their song selection is. Also ask for references from another event such as this they have done. Ask other organizations that have done similar events for suggestions on DJs.

- Host this at your own venue with other small events happening and use a karaoke machine.

59. Male Beauty Pageant

Description: Gather a group of brave males willing to dress up as ladies to help your cause. Hold a pageant during which men will compete for best talent, answer questions, and be judged on their dresses. Crown the winner and provide a sash and bouquet of flowers. Charge an admission fee.

Estimated Cost:

Levels of Difficulty:

Obtaining Sponsors/Donations	✪ ✪ ✪
Finding a Venue	✪ ✪
Recruiting Volunteers	✪ ✪
Preparation	✪ ✪ ✪ ✪
Execution	✪ ✪ ✪ ✪

Sponsor/Donation/Volunteer Tip(s):

- Find brave men willing to donate their time as a contestant.

- Ask women to lend their fancy dresses to the men for the evening. Meet at least a month in advance to have the participant try on the dress to make sure it fits well enough to wear.

- Have each participant seek a sponsor.

- You can sell also sponsorships of tables if you chose to serve lunch or dinner.

- Social halls, churches, schools and hotels are possible venues.

60. Movie Premiere

Description: Reserve seats in a large theater for the premiere of a highly-anticipated movie and sell tickets. This can be a big money-maker, depending on the popularity of the movie being premiered.

Estimated Cost:

Levels of Difficulty:

Obtaining Sponsors/Donations	⭐⭐⭐
Finding a Venue	⭐⭐⭐⭐
Recruiting Volunteers	⭐⭐
Preparation	⭐⭐
Execution	⭐⭐

Sponsors/Donations:

- A local business may sponsor your entire event by purchasing your tickets up-front. You will then sell all the tickets at a straight profit.

- If you can get the theater owner to donate the entire theater, all the better.

Execution Tip(s):

- Poll potential supporters to see what kinds of movies they prefer seeing so you can choose the movie that might attract the most people.

- See if the theater will allow you to sell your own concessions or receive a portion of the profit from the concessions sold the night of the event.

61. Superstar Idol Singing Show

Description: Do your own take on the popular American Idol singing show. Hold auditions, choose contestants, and find three judges who can imitate the personalities of the ones on the show and provide entertaining feedback. Sell tickets for admission. Then let audience members vote on ballots and announce the winner and runners-up with a special ceremony.

Estimated Cost:

Levels of Difficulty:

Obtaining Sponsors/Donations	★★
Finding a Venue	★★
Recruiting Volunteers	★★★
Preparation	★★★★★
Execution	★★★★★

Special Materials/Equipment:

- ☐ Sound equipment (microphone, speakers)
- ☐ Stage
- ☐ Music
- ☐ Seating

Sponsors/Donations:

- Find someone to donate a prize for the winner, like a travel agent who can donate a trip to Los Angeles to see American Idol.

- Ask local grocery stores and restaurants to donate baked goods and snacks that you can sell at the event.

- Your organization's home is a good venue for this kind of event. This event would be great in a school with an auditorium, gym, and/or cafeteria. If you do not have such a venue available to you, a local community theater makes for a nice alternative.

Execution Tip(s):

- Make sure that you are cleared to publicly play and perform any music that will be used during this event.

Variation(s):

- Do your own take on any popular competitive reality TV show for an evening of fun (i.e. So You Think You Can Dance, Top Chef, America's Next Top Model, The Bachelor, etc.).

62. Talent Show

Description: For an entry fee, participants can witness the talents of members in the community. Advertise for local talent early to get a wide variety of talents. Advertise for everything from musicians to "stupid human tricks." This variety of performances makes the event fun and memorable. Arrange for an array of quick concessions during intermission, like soda, hot dogs, candy, and popcorn.

Estimated Cost:

Levels of Difficulty:

Obtaining Sponsors/Donations	★ ★
Finding a Venue	★
Recruiting Volunteers	★ ★ ★
Preparation	★ ★ ★ ★ ★
Execution	★ ★ ★ ★ ★

Special Materials/Equipment:

☐ Sound equipment (microphone, speakers)

☐ Stage

☐ Seating

Sponsor/Donation/Volunteer Tip(s):

- Find someone to donate a prize for the winner.

- Ask local grocery stores and restaurants to donate baked goods and snacks that you can sell at the event.

- Your organization's headquarters is a good venue for this kind of event. This event would be great in a school with an auditorium, gym, and/or cafeteria. If you do not have such a venue available to you, a local community theater makes for a nice alternative.

Execution Tip(s):

- Have a designed pamphlet with information about the acts in the show, and account for space to thank and advertise sponsors.

63. Ticket Sales for Touring Shows

Description: Traveling shows such as plays or circuses offer great fundraising opportunities. Locate a touring company that is scheduled to stop in your area and purchase tickets for its events. Sell tickets at a higher price, and the difference in amounts will go toward your cause.

Estimated Cost:

Levels of Difficulty:

Obtaining Sponsors/Donations	⭐ ⭐ ⭐
Finding a Venue	N/A
Recruiting Volunteers	⭐ ⭐
Preparation	⭐ ⭐
Execution	⭐ ⭐

Sponsors/Donations:

- A local business may sponsor your entire event by purchasing your tickets up-front. You can then sell the tickets for a full profit.

- Find out what events will be visiting your community and what events will likely appeal to your supporters.

- Arrange with the producers of the group to hold choice seats for you, and to let you sell your unsold tickets back before a set time.

- Allow yourself as much time as possible to sell your tickets.

Execution Tip(s):

- Poll your supporters to see what kinds of events they prefer seeing before you reserve the tickets.

- Check the legal terms and conditions for the tickets before selling them at an increased price.

Variation(s):

- For a grand variation, sell a holiday travel package. Arrange with a travel agent and sell the travel packages for an amount higher than the travel agent sells them to you. You can arrange a London theater tour, an African safari, Alaskan cruise, etc.

64. Truck Show

Description: Ask community and organization members who own large vehicles like trucks, tractors, or earth-movers to park them at your venue. Kids will jump at the chance to see these large trucks and have a chance to hop in the driver's seat. Charge an admission fee, sell photographs, and have the owners available to answer questions.

Estimated Cost:

Levels of Difficulty:

Obtaining Sponsors/Donations	✪ ✪ ✪
Finding a Venue	✪ ✪
Recruiting Volunteers	✪ ✪
Preparation	✪ ✪ ✪
Execution	✪ ✪ ✪

Special Materials/Equipment:

☐ Large vehicles

Sponsor/Donation/Volunteer Tip(s):

- The best sponsors you can have for such an event are local trucking companies, construction companies, and fire houses.

- This event will call for a large, outdoor venue in an area with high traffic to attract people passing by, like your organization's parking lot (if it is large enough) or the parking lot of a large vehicle dealer, city park, or mall.

Execution Tip(s):

- Plan on a time of year when people enjoy being outside and there is a minimal chance of being rained out.

Variation(s):

- Have an Antique Truck Show.

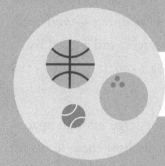

Sports

Sports naturally involve a high number of members and are an event people love to come watch and enjoy, making games a perfect way to fundraise. You can make extra profits by providing food and drink on game day as well.

Planning

Give yourself at least six months to plan the event, or even up to a year if possible. Planning a major event is like planning a big wedding — you need a venue, decorations, entertainment, food and beverages, and a guest list.

Sponsors

Look to the local recreational center and parks for large enough spaces and the proper equipment to sponsor and potentially host these kinds of events. Other local businesses and churches may also be good sponsors to seek funding for team uniforms or the like, since this provides a chance for them to be recognizably involved with their local community.

Volunteers

Volunteers will mostly be needed to referee, work concessions, and set up and break down the event. Around 10 to 15 volunteers should be sufficient to handle these tasks unless it is a larger game, or volunteers also participate in the sport, if so, try to attract as many volunteers as possible.

Venue

Recreation centers, parks, and land that have large, grassy fields available for use are ideal venue spaces for the average sport. If the sport is more specialized, consider what conditions you need to host the event and go from there. For instance, if the sport is ice hockey, you will need an ice rink or safely frozen lake.

Preparation

Start off by creating an executive committee that is responsible for major decisions about the auction and delegating work to other committees. Then move on to deciding the type of auction, deciding a venue, sponsors, and fundraising goals. Be confident when asking for donations or sponsorships and be clear in what you are fundraising for; this will make possible sponsors more inclined to help your cause.

From there you can move on to advertising the event to the community using social media, radio commercials, newspaper ads, flyers posted around busy areas of town, and other means. If you can, decide a target audience and cater to these people. It is more effective to directly appeal to a certain audience than trying to encompass the blanket term of 'everyone.' Target audiences can be based on almost anything, but age and location are easy to market to.

Always arrive early to set up the event, and account for time needed to break down and clean up the venue afterwards. For planned activities during the event, consider creating a script for the master of ceremonies to read. Be transparent about the items offered in the event, and do not advertise items that won't be sold or that you cannot guarantee will be sold on auction day. Ideally wait until you have several items and business sponsorships before advertising to the community.

65. Adventure Race

Description: Locate a venue with a large space and a variety of terrains or set up obstacles. Create a challenging and creative obstacle course for people to race through. Consider using a ropes course.

Estimated Cost:

Levels of Difficulty:

Obtaining Sponsors/Donations	★★★
Finding a Venue	★★★★
Recruiting Volunteers	★★★
Preparation	★★★★★
Execution	★★★★★

Special Materials/Equipment:

☐ A variety of structures to create safe obstacles.

Sponsors/Donations:

• Sports clubs with an emphasis on outdoor challenges.

Possible Venue(s):

• A local ropes course.

• A large park.

66. Boat Race

Description: Locate a venue to host a boating race and charge an entry fee for viewing and participating in the event. Provide prizes for race winners and offer concessions to spectators.

Estimated Cost:

Levels of Difficulty:

Obtaining Sponsors/Donations	★★★
Finding a Venue	★★★★
Recruiting Volunteers	★★★
Preparation	★★★★★
Execution	★★★★★

Special Materials/Equipment:

☐ Buoys (to mark the racecourse)

Sponsors/Donations:

- A local marina is a good choice for a sponsor in areas that are near larger bodies of water.

- Local outdoors clubs, sporting goods, and boating stores are also good sponsor possibilities.

- Have racers collect sponsorships in the same manner that they would in an event such as a walk-a-thon (see sample form and rules in Appendices).

Possible Venue(s): Your venue can range from a small farm pond to the Pacific Ocean and everything in between.

67. Fishing Tournament

Description: Participants will have a "reel" good time competing in a fishing tournament while you catch some profits. Gather corporate sponsors and provide prizes for the event.

Estimated Cost:

Levels of Difficulty:

Obtaining Sponsors/Donations	★ ★ ★
Finding a Venue	★ ★ ★
Recruiting Volunteers	★ ★
Preparation	★ ★ ★
Execution	★ ★ ★

Special Materials/Equipment:

☐ Fishing gear (poles, lures, bait, etc.)

Sponsors/Donations:

• Sporting goods stores are excellent sponsors for such events. Local sporting social clubs are also possible sponsors and may be able to help with equipment.

Possible Venue(s): A city park with a lake or river is a good venue. If you are in a location situated on a larger body of water, consider a pier, dock, or boat.

Tip(s):

- This event can be held any time of year if you are in a location where ice fishing is popular.

- Make additional profits by selling T-shirts or having a vendor fair.

68. Golf Tournament

Description: Give participants the opportunity to tee-off for a good cause.

Estimated Cost:

Levels of Difficulty:

Obtaining Sponsors/Donations	★ ★ ★
Finding a Venue	★ ★
Recruiting Volunteers	★ ★
Preparation	★ ★
Execution	★ ★

Sponsors/Donations:

- Try to find a company, business, or individual who can sponsor the entire event by covering greens fees for the tournament. That way, whatever the golfers give goes straight to your organization.

- Also consider finding people and businesses to sponsor a hole or a golfer's game. Each golfer can sign up sponsors that will pay a per-hole sponsorship pledge to the golfer. Pledges of $100 each for 18 holes will quickly add up.

- Attempt to get golf clubs, bags, and assorted golf related items donated to be bid on throughout the day in a silent auction.

Possible Venue(s): A public golf course or a country club will provide what you need.

Tip(s):

- Find a good course with many amenities. The nicer the course, the better turnout you will have.

- Get a golf pro to volunteer to attend as a way to advertise and attract more golfers.

Variation(s):

- Have a miniature golf tournament to attract family participation.

- A competition at a driving range.

69. Hot-Air Balloon Race

Description: Find a large, open field and gather several professional hot-air balloonists. Choose a day with favorable winds and comfortable temperatures. Possible areas for this event include a construction site of a shopping mall, large parks, farm fields, or lawns of estates. Charge a fee for watching the race, or take bets on balloons and obtain sponsorship on each balloon. Make additional profits by holding raffles, selling food, or selling pictures inside the balloon baskets.

Estimated Cost:

Levels of Difficulty:

Obtaining Sponsors/Donations	✪ ✪ ✪ ✪
Finding a Venue	✪ ✪ ✪
Recruiting Volunteers	✪ ✪
Preparation	✪ ✪ ✪ ✪
Execution	✪ ✪ ✪ ✪

Special Materials/Equipment:

☐ Hot-air balloons

Sponsors/Donations:

• Corporate sponsors who already sponsor your organization are likely to agree to serve as individual balloon sponsors and/or event sponsors.

Possible Venue(s): You need a large open area, such as a park, school field, or mall parking lot.

70. Mudfest

Description: People will gladly pay for a chance to play in the mud, or to watch the messy action from the sidelines — especially in a high school or college atmosphere. Create a mud pit by having a pit dug and filled with clay and water. Hold a week-long competition in which teams can pay to play mud games including mud tug, mud volleyball, mud polo, and mud Frisbee. Award trophies to the winning teams. Have T-shirt decorating contests, spirit points, and money wars. Hold a mud dance at the end of the games, complete with a DJ and an outdoor photo backdrop, and charge an admission fee.

Estimated Cost: $ $ $ $

Levels of Difficulty:

Obtaining Sponsors/Donations	★ ★ ★
Finding a Venue	★ ★ ★ ★
Recruiting Volunteers	★ ★
Preparation	★ ★ ★ ★ ★
Execution	★ ★ ★ ★ ★

Special Materials/Equipment:

☐ Mud pit (hire a backhoe to dig a pit, and have clay imported; add water)

☐ Hose or outdoor shower

☐ Volleyball and volleyball net

☐ Water polo ball and two goals

☐ Frisbee

☐ Tug-of-war rope

☐ Cones (to mark the "field")

☐ Whistles (for referees)

☐ Empty water or milk jugs (for the money wars)

Sponsors/Donations:

- This type of event is ideal for local beverage distributor sponsorships.

- Seek local sports stores to donate old sports equipment for the mud games.

- Try to find a DJ who would offer free services for the dance.

- Ask a T-shirt company to donate or give discounted custom-made shirts and offer sponsors advertising space on the back of the shirt.

Possible Venue(s): An ideal venue might be a large, grassy field in a convenient location for spectators and that you have permission to dig up. Make sure showers and hoses can be stationed nearby so contestants can wash off. Local county fairgrounds, where you might find arena seating around an open dirt floor normally used for rodeo shows, might work too.

Execution

1. Have everything set up before teams arrive to sign in.

2. Have volunteers sign teams in, collect submissions of T-shirt designs (or take a picture of the printed T-shirts), and show them the money jar that will be theirs to fill for the week for money wars.

3. Post a giant schedule up in an obvious place near the mud pit.

4. Charge spectators an entry fee, and let the games begin.

5. Start games on time and follow your script to carry out all planned activities.

6. Initiate cleanup at the designated end time.

Tip(s):

- Because the mud may be slippery, and sports activities involve a certain amount of risk, have all participants sign liability waivers.

Variation(s):

- Have a Snowfest and set up the same games in the snow (snow volleyball, snow tug, snow polo, and snow Frisbee) and of course, the traditional snowman-building contest. If it is in a place that does not get snow, import a heap of snow.

71. Rock Climbing

Description: Promote excitement and adventure by letting participants climb to the top of a rock wall for a fee.

Estimated Cost:

Levels of Difficulty:

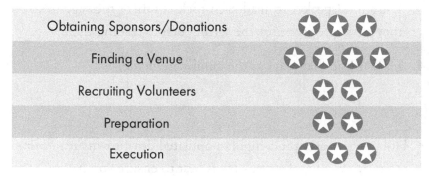

Obtaining Sponsors/Donations	★★★
Finding a Venue	★★★★
Recruiting Volunteers	★★
Preparation	★★
Execution	★★★

Special Materials/Equipment:

☐ Rock wall and climbing equipment

☐ Loudspeaker

☐ Music/sound equipment

Sponsors/Donations:

- Ask a rock climbing rental company to lend their climbing wall, equipment, and services for free or at a discount.

- Ask local food stores to donate snacks and beverages to sell to spectators.

Possible Venue(s): Consider a gym, basketball court, or field.

Execution:

1. Set up your equipment and refreshments, put out a sign to advertise to passersby, and start selling.

2. As people sign up to rock climb, have them write a message they would like read about themselves or to friends who are watching, and have them write how they might support your organization.

3. Use a loudspeaker to read each rock climber's message. Make sure they are appropriate for the setting before reading them.

4. Have music that plays as the climbs are made.

Tip(s):

- Holding this event in a highly populated downtown area during the early evening of a weekday is best to ensure you have a large audience. Friday evening at 5 p.m. is ideal.

- Though people will pay to rock climb, they can also get other donors to sponsor their activity. This is a good way to add additional donations.

- Some YMCAs have rock climbing walls and may be willing to host a charitable event.

72. Sky Diving

Description: Fundraising does not get much more thrilling than jumping out of a plane for a cause. Create a personal campaign on **www. skydive4free.com.** Once you collect $500 in donations, take a free jump for your organization. Encourage other friends and supporters of your cause to follow suit.

Estimated Cost:

Levels of Difficulty:

Obtaining Sponsors/Donations	⭐⭐⭐
Finding a Venue	⭐⭐
Recruiting Volunteers	⭐⭐⭐
Preparation	⭐⭐
Execution	⭐⭐

Sponsors/Donations:

- E-mail family and friends a letter asking them to donate to help reach your goal to help your organization and make the skydive happen. Send them a link to your fundraising account on **www. skydive4free.com**.

- Choose your fundraising goal. This organization will set you up online to start raising a minimum of $500 toward your free skydive. When a minimum of $500 is raised, an individual from your organization will take a tandem skydive (one during which the skydiver is attached to a skydive instructor) in support of your cause. The more money raised, the higher the percentage of funds your organization will receive. Based on the amount of $500, approximately 50 percent of your fund raising will go to your organization. A campaign raising $1,000 would see about 70 percent of the money pledged. If you raise $5,000, your organization would see about 90 percent of the money pledged.

Execution:

1. Once the fundraising goal is met, arrange to have someone from your organization jump from a plane with an instructor. Before you begin collecting donations, be sure that you have someone willing to actually follow through with the skydive.

2. Send contributors photographs of the jump or invite them to watch the jumper land.

Tip(s):

- Buy the DVD of the skydiver's experience and have a viewing party. Charge a few dollars each for organization members and the skydiver's friends to come watch. Sell drinks, popcorn, and other snacks. Get the next person to sign up and commit to a dive for your organization.

- Raffle off the skydiving experience to donors, to incentivize donations.

73. Soccer Tournament

Description: Let participants go for the goal while helping you meet your fundraising goal. Charge a fee for teams to enter a soccer tournament. You can also have a kicking competition to see who can make the most goals in a row or in a certain time period. Make sure to offer other activities for families during the event.

Estimated Cost:

Levels of Difficulty:

Obtaining Sponsors/Donations	✪ ✪ ✪
Finding a Venue	✪ ✪
Recruiting Volunteers	✪ ✪
Preparation	✪ ✪ ✪
Execution	✪ ✪ ✪

Special Materials/Equipment:

☐ Soccer equipment (goals, soccer balls)

Sponsors/Donations:

• Sporting goods stores are excellent sponsors for such events.

• Local sporting social clubs are also possible sponsors and may be able to help with equipment.

Possible Venue(s): City parks with soccer fields are good venues. Schools are also excellent places to hold such events.

Tip(s):

- A carnival can serve as a nice way to obtain additional profits for your organization.

Variation(s):

- Hold a baseball, softball, or wiffle ball tournament.

- Have a flag football tournament.

74. Water Sports Challenge

Description: Arrange for a local water sports center to provide a discount on morning or afternoon waterskiing or windsurfing. Obtain sponsors to donate to your charity based on the amount of time participants are able to stay standing. If some people are not avid water-skiers, in good spirits, have them seek sponsorship for the amount of times they fall.

Estimated Cost:

Levels of Difficulty:

Obtaining Sponsors/Donations	⭐⭐⭐
Finding a Venue	⭐⭐⭐⭐
Recruiting Volunteers	⭐⭐
Preparation	⭐⭐⭐
Execution	⭐⭐⭐

Sponsors/Donations:

- Find a water sports center to lend their equipment and facility.

- Seek sponsorships from local sporting goods stores or sports drink distributors.

Possible Venue(s): A good water sports center is key.

Tip(s):

- Most likely, you will raise the most funds by holding your event on a weekend. To get the most desirable date, you may have to pay the water sports center for the use of their facility and charge your supporters a fee that covers the cost of admission plus a donation to your organization.

- Most water sports centers have concession stands, so any food and drink that you plan to bring in will take business away from their concessions. Make arrangements regarding food and drink when you negotiate your facility usage.

 Themed Events

If your area has any unique qualities to it, utilize them to plan a themed event. Places near the coast have ample opportunities to plan beach-related activities while other cities have great historical buildings that can be used as great backdrops to a successful fundraising event.

Planning

Give yourself at least six months to plan the event, or even up to a year if possible. Planning a major event is like planning a big wedding — you need a venue, decorations, entertainment, food and beverages, and a guest list.

Sponsors

Consider asking a business to sponsor the entire event. Know what you can promise them. Offer to include their name or logo on event materials or link to their social media. Remember to further thank your sponsors during the actual event.

Volunteers

Depending on the kind of themed event you host, 10 to 15 or more volunteers should be sufficient to handle guests, serving food if needed, and making any other miscellaneous tasks needed throughout the event.

Venue

This will vary largely according to your specific fundraiser. First consider what the theme of the event entails and try to come up with an appropriate venue from there.

Preparation

Start off by creating an executive committee that is responsible for major decisions about the auction and delegating work to other committees.

Then move on to deciding the type of auction, deciding a venue, sponsors, and fundraising goals. Be confident when asking for donations or sponsorships and be clear in what you are fundraising for; this will make possible sponsors more inclined to help your cause.

From there you can move on to advertising the event to the community using social media, radio commercials, newspaper ads, flyers posted around busy areas of town, and other means. If you can, decide a target audience and cater to these people. It is more effective to directly appeal to a certain audience than trying to encompass the blanket term of 'everyone.' Target audiences can be based on almost anything, but age and location are easy to market to.

Always arrive early to set up the event, and account for time needed to break down and clean up the venue afterwards. For planned activities during the event, consider creating a script for the master of ceremonies to read. Be transparent about the items offered in the event, and do not advertise items that won't be sold or that you cannot guarantee will be sold on auction day. Ideally wait until you have several items and business sponsorships before advertising to the community.

75. Beach Bash

Description: This fundraiser is ideal for communities by the coast. Arrange for popular bands to perform and organize volleyball tournaments with entry costs and cash prizes for the winners. Hold a babes and hunks contest, and have people pay a small fee to cast their vote. Have a drink company provide refreshments at the event and get a local radio station to broadcast live from the beach to draw more people to attend.

Estimated Cost:

Levels of Difficulty:

Obtaining Sponsors/Donations	★ ★ ★
Finding a Venue	★ ★ ★ ★
Recruiting Volunteers	★ ★
Preparation	★ ★ ★ ★
Execution	★ ★ ★ ★

Special Materials/Equipment:

- ☐ Sound equipment (microphone, speakers)

- ☐ Stage (for live bands)

- ☐ Volleyball equipment

Sponsor/Donation/Volunteer Tip(s):

- Local sports drink distributors are perfect sponsors for these events. Ideally, you want sponsorship dollars to allow these sponsors to spread their names all over your event. They get advertising and you get their support.

- Have volunteers act as the referees to volleyball games and the master of ceremonies for the babes and hunks contest.

Execution Tip(s):

- Plan ahead to account for weather and have a backup event day in the works should the fundraiser get rained out.

76. Black Tie Gala

Description: Guests can enjoy a formal evening of dinner, a live jazz band, and a silent auction for luxurious experiences like spa retreats while you bring in the money from ticket sales.

Estimated Cost:

Levels of Difficulty:

Obtaining Sponsors/Donations	★ ★ ★ ★
Finding a Venue	★ ★ ★
Recruiting Volunteers	★ ★
Preparation	★ ★ ★
Execution	★ ★ ★

Sponsor/Donation/Volunteer Tip(s):

- Find a major supporter to sponsor the entire event or to cover the cost of the venue.

- Seek several sponsors for tables. A sponsor might purchase a table that seats 10 for dinner and give the tickets to employees, friends, or family.

- Have sponsors donate big-ticket items to auction for the silent auction, like trips, large electronics, or jewelry.

- A hotel is a great venue because it usually has a large ballroom, a caterer, and an in-house sound system and lighting.

Execution Tip(s):

- Send out a "save-the-date" card or email a month or two before the event. This card will let people know the purpose of the event, date, place, and maybe even what entertainment might be featured. The trick with the save-the-date card is to send it out early enough to give your potential audience the heads-up about your event, but not so early that they will forget about it.

77. Casino Night

Description: Go "all in" on his fun evening of casino games. Casino nights are popular and simple to promote, so it is a safe bet that your organization will be successful. Consider making it into an annual occurrence.

Estimated Cost: $ $ $ $

Levels of Difficulty:

Obtaining Sponsors/Donations	★ ★ ★
Finding a Venue	★ ★ ★
Recruiting Volunteers	★ ★ ★
Preparation	★ ★ ★ ★
Execution	★ ★ ★ ★

Special Materials/Equipment:

- ☐ Casino games
- ☐ Card tables
- ☐ Chairs
- ☐ Multiple decks of playing cards
- ☐ Poker chips

Sponsor/Donation/Volunteer Tip(s):

- Ask party supply houses if you can rent games and chips for free or for a reduced price. Many cities also have companies that will offer equipment and personnel to assist you in your event.

- Solicit sponsors and items for auction and arrange plans for a catered dinner.

- Try to find a company, business, or individual that may sponsor the entire event. The sponsorship cost could cover the cost of the venue and any rentals you may have to obtain to outfit the venue.

- Each player can sign up sponsors to pay a per-game sponsorship pledge to the player or simply pledge the player's evening.

- Consider finding people and businesses to sponsor a game (such as a roulette sponsor) or a card table. For instance, you might be able to get 20 sponsors to donate $100 per game.

- Try getting donations of cash or big-ticket items such as flat-screen TVs or even a car that will be used for a silent auction or raffle at the event.

- A casino, hotel, recreation room, or any place that has the space and permits gambling is good for a venue.

Execution Tip(s):

- Events such as these are good for utilizing many different ways of raising funds. If you begin planning early, you can include a poker tournament, silent auction, and raffle.

- Set up side tables that people can buy into when they get eliminated from their original card game table. This is a good way to make a few extra dollars and it keeps people at your event from beginning to end.

78. Fabulous New York Fundraiser

Description: Have guests take a trip to New York without the expense of traveling. Sell tickets for admission to the event. Decorate your venue with skyscrapers backdrops, bright lights, billboards, city street signs, and maybe even a few taxi cabs (or pictures of them).

Estimated Cost:

Levels of Difficulty:

Obtaining Sponsors/Donations	★★
Finding a Venue	★★
Recruiting Volunteers	★★
Preparation	★★★
Execution	★★★

Special Materials/Equipment:

☐ New York decorations

☐ Banquet tables and chairs

☐ Sound system (microphone, speakers)

Sponsor/Donation/Volunteer Tip(s):

- The best donation that you might possibly get is an event or venue sponsor. Otherwise, seek sponsors for each banquet table.

- If you want to go all out, have the event at an upscale hotel in your community or any venue with a fancy banquet room.

Execution Tip(s)

- Have New York associated events happen throughout the night such as standup comedy, short "Broadway" skits, and other stereotypically New York style activities.

Variation(s):

☐ Hold a Foggy London Fundraiser.

79. Go Green Party

Description: This hot topic is a cool way to help the earth while raising money for your organization. Gather a group of friends and start a community beautification initiative. Have volunteers and supporters of your efforts make donations to your organization. Host a party featuring a premier of a popular nature program and educate participants about smarter living habits. Have computers set up at the party, and encourage people to email local, state, and federal officials, campaigning for a greener tomorrow.

Estimated Cost:

Levels of Difficulty:

Obtaining Sponsors/Donations	✪✪
Finding a Venue	✪✪
Recruiting Volunteers	✪✪
Preparation	✪✪✪
Execution	✪✪✪

Special Materials/Equipment:

Depending on the beautification project you choose, you may need:

☐ Trash bags

☐ Gloves

☐ Sandblaster (for graffiti)

☐ Paint

☐ Plants

☐ Shovels

For party:

☐ Sound equipment (microphone, speakers)

☐ Lighting

☐ Educational materials/video

☐ Projection equipment

☐ Computers

Sponsor/Donation/Volunteer Tip(s):

- Local environmental groups might be good sponsors for this event.

- Also, if there is a local business that markets itself as a supporter of environmental issues, you might try speaking to them about sponsoring your event.

- If you are planning on your event taking place during warmer months, consider holding your event outside in a city park. If your event is at a time of the year when you are better off planning for an indoor party, choose a place where you can best highlight your message.

Variation(s):

- Have the party after completing the beautification project. Sell tickets at a discounted price to those who participated in the project. Beautification could include renting a sandblaster to erase graffiti from buildings; picking up litter from a street, beach, park, or your organization's parking lot; painting old buildings; and doing landscaping.

80. Harry Potter Extravaganza

Description: Host a Harry Potter themed party, and watch your guests light up with excitement as they enter this fantasy world. Ask a local magician to perform and teach guests tricks and magic spells at a magic-themed bar. Cover your venue with wizard decorations and other pictures in the Harry Potter theme. Have guests dress up as their favorite Harry Potter character. Charge an admission fee.

Estimated Cost:

Levels of Difficulty:

Obtaining Sponsors/Donations	⭐⭐⭐
Finding a Venue	⭐⭐⭐⭐
Recruiting Volunteers	⭐⭐
Preparation	⭐⭐⭐⭐
Execution	⭐⭐⭐⭐

Special Materials/Equipment:

☐ Hogwarts decorations

☐ Harry Potter themed food service items like non-alcoholic butter beer, treacle tarts, and chocolate frogs

Sponsor/Donation/Volunteer Tip(s):

• Local theaters and performing arts organizations or theatrical prop companies are great places to seek donations of costumes and props for this event.

- Local bookstores may also be good places to seek sponsorships.

- Large old churches, community buildings, or schools could be good venues.

Execution Tip(s):

- Be aware that Harry Potter is a copyrighted character and you should only use the names and likenesses of the popular characters in ways that are not in violation of copyright laws.

Variation(s):

- For those who prefer vampires and werewolves, try hosting a Twilight Party.

81. International Day

Description: Celebrate diversity by hosting a day featuring food, music, and speakers from around the world.

Estimated Cost:

Levels of Difficulty:

Obtaining Sponsors/Donations	★★★
Finding a Venue	★★
Recruiting Volunteers	★★
Preparation	★★★★
Execution	★★★★

Special Materials/Equipment:

☐ International food

☐ International decorations (i.e. flags, travel brochures)

☐ International music

Sponsor/Donation/Volunteer Tip(s):

- Many larger urban areas have international consulates or representatives that may wish to sponsor your event.

- Many cultural groups have social organizations committed to helping the community-at-large better understand their cultures by sponsoring the event.

- Social halls, churches, schools, and hotels are possible venues.

Variation(s):

- Theme the night around one country, such as by having an Italian Spaghetti Dinner and Opera, or an Evening in Ireland featuring a band that plays Irish jigs and waltzes.

- Plan an International Speakers Dinner featuring speakers from a variety of countries.

82. Medieval Feast

Description: Host a banquet at which silverware is a foreign concept! Instead of fancy dishes, serve classic finger foods like chicken wings and other forms of meat, and maybe even a whole roast pig and some ale. Decorate with armor, weapons, and pictures of knights and dragons. Encourage guests to dress in their best medieval fare. Charge a fee for admission and dinner.

Estimated Cost:

Levels of Difficulty:

Obtaining Sponsors/Donations	★★★
Finding a Venue	★★★★★
Recruiting Volunteers	★★
Preparation	★★★★★
Execution	★★★★★

Special Materials/Equipment:

- ☐ Medieval decorations
- ☐ Medieval-style dinner food
- ☐ Long tables
- ☐ Chairs

Sponsor/Donation/Volunteer Tip(s):

- Local theaters and performing arts organizations are suitable places to seek donations of costumes and props.

- Large old churches, community buildings, or schools make for good locations.

Variation(s):

- Hold a Roman Toga Banquet.

- Have a Western Chuck Wagon Scrounge.

83. Murder Mystery Party

Description: Invite guests to enjoy the thrill of a meal during which a murder takes place and they must figure out who the culprit is. Prepare a series of staged scenes and plant evidence around the venue. Have volunteers dress up as characters in the scenario or encourage guests to take on the guise of the characters in the murder mystery by secretly assigning roles to each guest prior to the event so they have time to prepare.

Estimated Cost:

Levels of Difficulty:

Obtaining Sponsors/Donations	✪✪✪
Finding a Venue	✪✪✪✪
Recruiting Volunteers	✪✪
Preparation	✪✪✪✪✪
Execution	✪✪✪✪✪

Special Materials/Equipment:

☐ Appropriate decorations for the kind of space you want the murder to take place in (a hotel, home, school, etc.)

☐ Evidence props such as the weapon, finger prints, and other clues.

Sponsors/Donations:

• Local theaters and performing arts organizations are suitable places to seek donations of costumes and props.

Possible Venue(s): Large old churches, community buildings, or schools make for good locations.

84. Night in Paris

Description: Revive the romantic vibes of Paris by hosting a French dinner. For a set admission fee, guests can enjoy fine French cuisine, such as French bread, cheese, and wine. Decorate the venue with items reminiscent of Paris, like an Eiffel Tower replica and pictures of the city.

Estimated Cost:

Levels of Difficulty:

Obtaining Sponsors/Donations	⭐⭐
Finding a Venue	⭐⭐
Recruiting Volunteers	⭐⭐
Preparation	⭐⭐⭐
Execution	⭐⭐⭐

Special Materials/Equipment:

☐ Parisian decorations

☐ French food

☐ Banquet tables

☐ Chairs

☐ Sound system (microphone, speakers)

☐ Specialty lighting

☐ Candles (or depending upon your venue, fake candles)

Sponsors/Donations:

- The best donation is that of a venue.

- Seek out event sponsors.

- Find sponsors for each banquet table.

Possible Venue(s): Consider having it at an upscale hotel in your community, or at any venue with a fancy banquet room.

85. Picture Perfect Party

Description: Guests at this fundraising event will have the opportunity to be captured in unique photo settings. Recreate movie scenes in your venue where guests can feel like true stars and have their photos taken. Be sure to include great food, and even an auction for valuable items that once belonged to celebrities. Have drama clubs in the community help create props and scenery and make this event a night to remember. Charge a fee for general admission.

Estimated Cost:

Levels of Difficulty:

Obtaining Sponsors/Donations	⭐⭐⭐⭐
Finding a Venue	⭐⭐⭐
Recruiting Volunteers	⭐⭐
Preparation	⭐⭐⭐⭐⭐
Execution	⭐⭐⭐⭐⭐

Special Materials/Equipment:

☐ Sets

☐ Props

☐ Costumes

☐ Photography equipment

Sponsors/Donations:

- A professional photographer and a local theater company can offer valuable assistance.

Possible Venue(s): Schools, churches, social clubs or any large open space where you can have a variety of things happening at the same time will work well for this event. Ideally, choose a venue that you have access to 24 hours in advance. It is important that your scenery and items associated with your photo shoots are in place and ready to go before you open your doors.

Tip(s):

- Consider doing this event in the fall and staging a Grinch or Christmas Story scene. Offering to help people take care of their holiday card needs is a good incentive to bring people to your event.

86. Renaissance Fair

Description: Have guests dress in attire from the renaissance era while enjoying all the elements of the time period. Host games and activities and charge a fee to participate. Set a price to dine without silverware and watch as your guests let loose.

Estimated Cost:

Levels of Difficulty:

Obtaining Sponsors/Donations	★★★
Finding a Venue	★★
Recruiting Volunteers	★★
Preparation	★★★★★
Execution	★★★★★

Special Materials/Equipment:

- ☐ Renaissance costumes
- ☐ Props

Sponsors/Donations:

- Contact local businesses to act as event sponsors. Set sponsorship levels and offer potential sponsors advertising rights and other perks to make sponsorship attractive.

Possible Venue(s): A park with natural amphitheater is ideal because it will allow you to have a renaissance performance in a natural setting while not having to worry about bringing seating in.

87. Spa Day

Description: Have participants relax and get pampered during a fundraising event at a spa, salon, barbershop, or beauty vocational school. Beauticians can commit to donating a portion of their proceeds for a day or a specified number of hours to your cause. Supporters can receive a wide range of treatments, including manicures, foot treatments, massages, hair treatments, and facials.

Estimated Cost:

Levels of Difficulty:

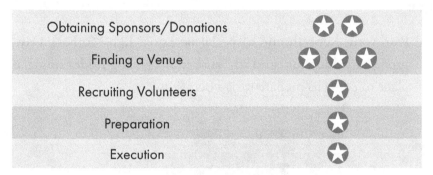

Obtaining Sponsors/Donations	✪ ✪
Finding a Venue	✪ ✪ ✪
Recruiting Volunteers	✪
Preparation	✪
Execution	✪

Special Materials/Equipment: N/A

Sponsors/Donations:

- Approach beauty supply stores, women's apparel stores, nail salons, and other beauty-related businesses to donate cash or services in exchange for publicity during the event.

- Ideally, you would like a high-end spa to sponsor your event. You can sell tickets for admission to the spa, and the spa will draw people in that have never been there and make money from the sale of spa items such as soaps, lotions, and oils. If you plan your event for a time that is considered an "off time" for the spa and you can offer them a full house of your supporters that may become new spa patrons, they will likely be more than happy to do the event.

- Other great donations toward this event would be a variety of soaps, lotions, and bath oils to use as gifts or raffle items.

Possible Venue(s): Hair salons, barbershops, and beauty vocational schools are appropriate. A mall or shopping center might also be willing to donate space where stylists can work, which would give the event great visibility to passersby.

Tip(s):

- Plan your event around a special occasion, like Mother's Day, prom, or graduation, and advertise it as a great gift idea or great place to come to prepare for an occasion.

Variation(s):

- Suggest that the salon staff offer mini services, like a 15-minute hair trim, at a discount off the standard, full-service rate. That way, the stylists (who often are self-employed) will be able to perform more services while donating to your cause.

88. Superhero Fair

Description: Whether held indoors or outdoors, this fundraiser will be a hit for all ages. Charge a fee for admission to the event, and offer activities geared toward superhero themes, like a contest for who can hit closest to a target with silly string (Spider-Man), a cape-decorating station (Superman), superhero face painting, and a costume contest for which kids dress up as their favorite superhero. Provide treats and prizes fit for a superhero for winners of the games.

Estimated Cost: $ $ $ $

Levels of Difficulty:

Obtaining Sponsors/Donations	⭐⭐⭐
Finding a Venue	⭐
Recruiting Volunteers	⭐⭐⭐
Preparation	⭐⭐⭐⭐
Execution	⭐⭐⭐⭐

Special Materials/Equipment:

☐ Superhero decorations

☐ Game equipment

☐ Face paint

Sponsors/Donations:

- Ask party supply stores to donate superhero-themed toys and decorations.

Possible Venue(s): Your organization's home parking lot or a field is a great venue, whether your organization is a church, a school, or a community center.

89. Toga Party

Description: Bring the Roman Empire back to life with a toga party. Sell tickets before the event and ask that all guests show up dressed in togas. For dinner, offer a buffet served from a banquet table located at the center of your venue. Sell laurel wreaths to top off participants' outfits. Hold a contest for most unique toga (table cloth or bedsheets), most authentic toga, etc.

Estimated Cost:

Levels of Difficulty:

Obtaining Sponsors/Donations	★ ★ ★
Finding a Venue	★ ★ ★ ★
Recruiting Volunteers	★ ★
Preparation	★ ★ ★ ★
Execution	★ ★ ★ ★

Special Materials/Equipment:

☐ Roman decorations

☐ Food service items

Sponsors/Donations:

• Local theaters, performing arts organizations, and theatrical companies might be great places to seek donations of costumes and props for this event.

Possible Venue(s): Large old churches, community buildings, or schools are good venues.

Tip(s):

- Hold a toga-decorating contest and supply markers, buttons, sequins, ribbons, etc.

Variation(s):

- Have a White Night where everyone wears white.

- Host an Olympics Party modeled after ancient Olympic games and outfits.

90. '20s Dinner Party

Description: Travel back in time to the roaring '20s for a fun night of flapper dresses, fedoras, fine food, silent movies, and poker or craps games. Participants can take pictures in a photo booth or have Polaroids taken to take home as keepsakes. Teach guests a popular dance from the era, like the Charleston. Charge a general admission fee as well as small cost for taking pictures

Estimated Cost:

Levels of Difficulty:

Obtaining Sponsors/Donations	✪ ✪ ✪
Finding a Venue	✪ ✪ ✪
Recruiting Volunteers	✪ ✪
Preparation	✪ ✪ ✪
Execution	✪ ✪ ✪

Special Materials/Equipment:

- ☐ '20s decorations

- ☐ '20s music

- ☐ Sound system (microphone, speakers)

- ☐ Dance floor

- ☐ Silent movie and projector

- ☐ Poker or craps games

☐ Tables and chairs

☐ Photo booth and Polaroid camera

Sponsors/Donations:

- A local historical society might be a good place to begin looking for sponsorships and donations to use for the evening.

Possible Venue(s): A '20s-era hotel, social building, or hotel in your community might be the perfect venue.

Variation(s):

- You can have a dinner party celebrating another popular era, like the '70s or '80s.

91. Without a Clue Party

Description: In this interactive fundraiser, guests will be clueless as to why they are there. Leave clues in different areas of the venue that point to the purpose of the event. For example, place plant sticks in centerpieces with clues, or put more hints on napkins and underneath plates. Provide each guest with a mini spyglass as a party favor and decorate tables with question mark shaped candles. Charge guests an admission fee.

Estimated Cost:

Levels of Difficulty:

Obtaining Sponsors/Donations	⭐⭐
Finding a Venue	⭐⭐
Recruiting Volunteers	⭐⭐
Preparation	⭐⭐⭐
Execution	⭐⭐⭐

Special Materials/Equipment:

- ☐ Decorations and clues
- ☐ Banquet tables and chairs
- ☐ Sound system (microphone, speakers)

Sponsors/Donations:

- The best donation that you might possibly get is an event sponsor, or at least a venue sponsor or sponsors for each banquet table.

Possible Venue(s): Consider having it at an upscale hotel in your community, or any venue that may have a fancy banquet room.

Miscellaneous

This next section is for all of the possible fundraising events that are more standalone and don't really fit into a category. Don't let that discourage you from trying them out, though. These events can be anything from a craft fair to a fortune telling booth and are equally rewarding ways to fundraise for your organization.

Planning

Give yourself at least six months to plan the event, or even up to a year if possible. Planning a major event is like planning a big wedding — you need a venue, decorations, entertainment, food and beverages, and a guest list.

Sponsors

Consider asking a business to sponsor the entire event. Know what you can promise them. Offer to include their name or logo on event materials or link to their social media. Remember to further thank your sponsors during the actual event.

Volunteers

Depending upon the kind of event you host, 5 to15 volunteers should be sufficient to handle guests, advertising, selling tickets, or any other tasks you should need.

Venue

This also largely depends on the event, but hotels or country clubs with large banquet halls are typically nice places to start.

Preparation

Start off by creating an executive committee that is responsible for major decisions about the auction and delegating work to other committees.

Then move on to deciding the type of auction, deciding a venue, sponsors, and fundraising goals. Be confident when asking for donations or sponsorships and be clear about what you are fundraising for; this will make possible sponsors more inclined to help your cause.

From there you can move on to advertising the event to the community using social media, radio commercials, newspaper ads, flyers posted around busy areas of town, and other means. If you can, decide a target audience and cater to these people. It is more effective to directly appeal to a certain audience than trying to encompass the blanket term of 'everyone.' Target audiences can be based on almost anything, but age and location are easy to market to.

Always arrive early to set up the event, and account for time needed to break down and clean up the venue afterwards. For planned activities during the event, consider creating a script for the master of ceremonies to read. Be transparent about the items offered in the event, and do not advertise items that won't be sold or that you cannot guarantee will be sold on auction day. Ideally wait until you have several items and business sponsorships before advertising to the community.

92. Cash-for-Jewelry Party

Description: Provide participants with the opportunity to sell old or broken jewelry they no longer wear. Excited guests can will watch as their unwanted gold, silver, and platinum jewelry is tested, weighed, valued, and purchased by an appraiser from a company like American Gold & Diamond Buyers. Your organization receives 10 percent of the total purchase, everyone leaves richer, and no one has to buy anything.

Estimated Cost:

Levels of Difficulty:

Obtaining Sponsors/Donations	⭐
Finding a Venue	⭐ ⭐
Recruiting Volunteers	⭐ ⭐
Preparation	⭐ ⭐
Execution	⭐ ⭐

Special Materials/Equipment: NA

Sponsors/Donations:

- Find a jeweler with an appraiser who is willing to come to your event and give your organization a percentage of the total value of the metal it buys from your guests.

Possible Venue(s): You can do this at someone's home or you can arrange for a larger gathering and a dinner at a hotel or restaurant.

Execution

1. Let the appraiser buy guests' jewelry.

2. Serve food and run additional planned activities.

3. Receive a check from American Gold & Diamond Buyers for 10 percent of the total purchase from the event.

Tip(s):

- To raise even more money, charge an event admission fee.

93. Community Cleanup

Description: Promote your organization as a community steward and collect money for your good works at the same time with a garbage collection effort. Have community members sponsor participants by pledging a set price (from 1 cent up) for every piece of trash that participants collect. Tidy up a neighborhood, park, beach, or business district.

Estimated Cost:

Levels of Difficulty:

Obtaining Sponsors/Donations	⭐⭐⭐
Finding a Venue	⭐
Recruiting Volunteers	⭐⭐⭐
Preparation	⭐⭐
Execution	⭐⭐

Special Materials/Equipment:

- ☐ Garbage bags
- ☐ Gloves
- ☐ Brooms
- ☐ Sand-blaster (for graffiti)
- ☐ Tally sheets (for each volunteer to record the amount of garbage collected)

Sponsors/Donations:

- Have each volunteer find sponsors to donate money for each hour of cleaning the volunteer commits to and completes.

- Ask people to donate a certain amount of money for each bag of trash (or can, bottle, or piece of refuse) collected.

- Ask a local hardware store or store to donate supplies. Be sure to recognize them as sponsors during your activity.

- Collect additional sponsors during the vent by setting out a table or booth near your clean up with information about your organization.

- Consider taking sponsorship pledges on your website.

Possible Venue(s): Parks, urban neighborhoods, school grounds, scenic drives, or beaches are all possible locations. Your efforts will be welcomed in plenty of community places.

Tip(s):

- Remind volunteers to try not to disturb the people occupying the area you are cleaning.

- Bring brooms and dustpans to sweep up glass and unsanitary refuse.

94. Craft Fair

Description: Showcase a variety of crafts and charge exhibitioners a fee to set up a booth at the event. Sell tickets for admission, and offer other fundraising activities at the fair, such as bake sales or raffles.

Estimated Cost:

Levels of Difficulty:

Obtaining Sponsors/Donations	⭐ ⭐ ⭐
Finding a Venue	⭐ ⭐ ⭐
Recruiting Volunteers	⭐ ⭐
Preparation	⭐ ⭐ ⭐
Execution	⭐ ⭐ ⭐

Special Materials/Equipment:

☐ Tables or booths (to display the crafts)

Sponsors/Donations:

• Identify a corporate or business sponsor to cover the venue cost and/or the cost of display materials. Craft dealers are often good places to go for such support.

Possible Venue(s): Nice hotels that offer large banquet rooms accommodate such a need in terms of space and possible catering. For an outdoor event, try city parks or town squares. If you are going to be showing high-end crafts, be sure that you offer the craft artisans and dealers a secure venue.

Tip(s):

- To appeal to the craft artisans and dealers, offer to pass along any mailing list you generate from this event.

- Also, meet with the craft artisans and dealers individually to work out any marketing hooks that will help you to advertise your event and their items.

- Consider offering a wide selection of crafts — a little something for everyone — to increase the appeal of the show and increase the likelihood that the craft artisans and dealers will find new customers.

95. Designer Home Display

Description: Locate an empty home and contact several interior designers. Each will provide a new design for one room. Charge participants for home viewings and increase profits by hosting an opening night preview to the home for special guests with a luncheon or auction. You can also provide guests a chance to meet with the designers for tips for their homes.

Estimated Cost:

Levels of Difficulty:

Obtaining Sponsors/Donations	★★★
Finding a Venue	★★★★
Recruiting Volunteers	★★★
Preparation	★★★★★
Execution	★★★★★

Special Materials/Equipment:

☐ Paint, art, and other furnishings requested by the designers

Sponsors/Donations:

• An upscale home realtor who will help you find a choice home that is the right style and size for your event is the ideal sponsor.

Possible Venue(s): Find an empty house with design potential in a convenient location.

Tip(s):

- Do not forget to recognize and promote the design team and thank the owner of the property.

- Remember: the larger the home, the higher your costs will be. Be sure that your team understands the agreement with the owner of the property and leaves the property as requested.

96. Donate Your Vehicle

Description: Whether that old car that you want to get rid of is running or not, Donation Line will rev up a donation for your organization by auctioning it off. One of the largest vehicle donation centers in America, Donation Line auctions donated vehicles and gives your organization a percentage of the sales. The center also accepts trucks, boats, RVs, motorcycles, jet skis, and snowmobiles. Donors are compensated with IRS tax deduction documentation.

Estimated Cost:

Levels of Difficulty:

Obtaining Sponsors/Donations	★ ★ ★ ★
Finding a Venue	N/A
Recruiting Volunteers	★
Preparation	★
Execution	★

Special Materials/Equipment:

☐ Used vehicles

Sponsors/Donations:

• Contact supporters, volunteers, members of your organization, and used vehicle vendors for donations.

Possible Venue(s): N/A

Preparation:

1. Log on to **www.DonationLine.com** for easy instructions and copy-ready fliers about the program.

2. Register online by providing your organization's information. Donation Line will review your information and contact you.

3. Advertise by sending emails and letters, posting fliers, putting a notice on your organization's website, and making an announcement in your newsletter. Send press releases to local media outlets like newspapers and magazines and contact local TV news and radio stations to request coverage and publicity.

Execution:

1. Refer supporters to **www.DonationLine.com** to donate their vehicles and name your organization as the beneficiary.

2. Once the donated vehicles have been auctioned, you will receive a portion of the sales.

97. Flea Market

Description: Offer a range of booths featuring everything from jewelry to art to fresh fruit. People will be attracted to the market for its bargain prices and unique offerings. Set up concession stands throughout the venue to increase profits.

Estimated Cost:

Levels of Difficulty:

Obtaining Sponsors/Donations	★ ★ ★
Finding a Venue	★ ★ ★
Recruiting Volunteers	★ ★
Preparation	★ ★ ★ ★
Execution	★ ★ ★ ★

Special Materials/Equipment:

☐ Booths, tables, or other means to display goods

Sponsor/Donation/Volunteer Tip(s):

• Find a corporate or business sponsor to cover the venue cost and/or the cost of display equipment.

• Consider inviting local folk, jazz, or blues musicians to play for a passing of the hat.

• City parks and town squares can be ideal outdoor venues for a flea market. You can also have it in your organization's parking lot.

Execution Tip(s):

- Meet with the vendors individually well in advance of your event to work out any marketing hooks that will help you to market your event and help them to market their items. Do everything you can to make this a win/win event for your organization as well as the vendors.

- Offer a little something for everyone to increase the appeal of the market and increase the likelihood that the vendors will find new customers.

98. Fortune-Telling Fun

Description: Your organization will foretell a memorable fundraiser in its future by hiring a fortune-teller, astrologer, or tarot card, palm, or tealeaf reader. Charge guests for each fortune told. Set up an area for each reader and create appropriate lighting and other special effects at each table. Candles and black lights can also be used to increase the effects.

Estimated Cost: $ $ $ $

Levels of Difficulty:

Obtaining Sponsors/Donations	✪ ✪ ✪ ✪
Finding a Venue	✪ ✪
Recruiting Volunteers	✪ ✪
Preparation	✪ ✪ ✪
Execution	✪ ✪

Special Materials/Equipment:

☐ Mystical decorations

☐ Tarot cards, a crystal ball, or tea leaves (depending on the activity)

Sponsor/Donation/Volunteer Tip(s):

- Try getting a fortune-teller, astrologer, or tarot card, palm, or tea leaf reader to donate his/her services.

- Contact a local bar and ask that they donate the venue to your organization for an evening. Generally, you will charge admission to the bar and the bar will make money on the liquor sales. You can make other arrangements with the bar, such as increasing the price of drinks and you getting a percentage of drink sales, but you have to make it attractive to them, as well. If you plan your event for a night that is considered an "off night" for the bar, such as a Monday or Tuesday, and you can guarantee them a full house of your supporters, they will be more than happy to do the event.

- Select what other activities will occur at your event. You may want a live or silent auction, raffle, or band.

Execution Tip(s):

- Plan whether to have fortune-tellers go from table to table offering to tell the fortunes or set up in specific locations for your supporters to sit with them. If you are in a venue with a quiet back room, see if you can arrange for several séance sessions or past-life readings.

Variation(s):

- Host a Magic Night featuring magicians.

- Have a Hypnotist Night and get your message across in a humorous way ("Donate to the cause!").

99. Historic Home Tours

Description: Provide participants the chance to tour historic homes or other establishments in unique neighborhoods. Charge a fee for admission to the tour. Offer a program book to supporters.

Estimated Cost:

Levels of Difficulty:

Obtaining Sponsors/Donations	★★★
Finding a Venue	★★★★★
Recruiting Volunteers	★★★
Preparation	★★★★
Execution	★★★★★

Special Materials/Equipment:

☐ Bus or other large vehicle (to transport groups of people from place to place), unless you choose to offer a walking tour

☐ Catalogue that includes information about the historic homes

Sponsor/Donation/Volunteer Tip(s):

• Sponsors may include realtors, historical societies, and neighborhood associations.

• Find numerous historical venues (homes or buildings) located reasonably close together.

Execution Tip(s):

- Be in contact with all involved parties the day of the event before it begins. It is also wise to have some sort of communication plan set up so that you can let the home owners know when you are on your way.

- Have a member of your organization stay at the point of departure and be reachable all through the event, especially if you are doing multiple tours.

- Follow your script to carry out all planned activities.

- Let the volunteer at the point of departure know when you are on your way back. This will allow for greater hospitality, as will letting those waiting to go on the tour know that you are running on time. This is important especially if you are managing with one bus or a single walking tour.

100. Park Day

Description: Organize a barbecue in your community park for locals, and host fun games like flag football, Frisbee, tug-of-war, sack races, water balloon tosses, and more. In addition to being a fundraiser, this event is easily a "friend-raiser" for your organization.

Estimated Cost:

Levels of Difficulty:

Obtaining Sponsors/Donations	⭐⭐⭐
Finding a Venue	⭐⭐
Recruiting Volunteers	⭐⭐
Preparation	⭐⭐⭐
Execution	⭐⭐⭐

Special Materials/Equipment:

☐ Sound equipment (microphone, speakers)

☐ Game/activity equipment (i.e. football, Frisbee, rope, etc.)

Sponsor/Donation/Volunteer Tip(s):

- Ask attendees to bring a dish to share for a potluck meal or ask local vendors for food donations for the event.

- Try for some kind of media sponsorship. Radio stations are good places to start, and they will bring in music for dancing. They may consider doing live remote broadcasts from your event.

- Ideally, find a local park with large, open grassy areas for games and a pavilion for a place to eat and some shelter from the sun and rain. A large parking lot works as well.

Execution Tip(s):

- Consider having community teams to pay a fee to sign up to play in a mini sports tournament during the event.

Variation(s):

- Host a block party on your street and invite neighbors to participate.

- Create games of chance at which people can donate a certain amount (like $1 per turn) for a chance to participate.

- Invite community members to showcase their antique cars in a designated area for a fee. Offer prizes for oldest car, best in show, etc.

101. Play with a Puppy/Cuddle with a Cat

Description: Ask your local puppy shelter to rent out puppies for a few hours. Explain your cause and that you will be offering people in the community a chance to play with the puppies. Set up a table or booth at a school or park and offer puppy playtime for $5 per 30 minutes. Make sure all animals are leashed and vaccinated.

Estimated Cost:

Levels of Difficulty:

Obtaining Sponsors/Donations	⭐ ⭐
Finding a Venue	⭐ ⭐
Recruiting Volunteers	⭐ ⭐
Preparation	⭐ ⭐
Execution	⭐ ⭐

Special Materials/Equipment:

☐ Dog leashes

☐ Toys

☐ Booth equipment

Sponsor/Donation/Volunteer Tip(s):

• Local pet stores, humane societies, and/or pet supply outlets are all potential sponsors for this event. Offer the puppy supplier a good bit of positive advertising for participating.

- A city park with a good amount of foot traffic would be an ideal venue for this event.

- Either have volunteers bring their dogs or contact local animal shelters to ask to borrow their dogs.

Execution Tip(s):

- Arrange a way for the puppies or kittens to be transported to and from the venue space.

- If the dogs are available for adoption, consider working along with the dog supplier to adopt out the dogs and gain an additional profit through the adoption fees.

- When you put your booth together, be sure that you have a complete enclosure and that all of your puppies are leashed. You do not want to lose or have to chase any of your furry charges.

- Bring poop bags and be sure to clean up after the puppies.

Bibliography

Chandler, Krista. "Winner Named in Support Our Schools Car Raffle." Lompoc Record, Lompoc Record, 13 Dec. 2016, lompocrecord.com/ news/local/winner-named-in-support-our-schools-car-raffle/article_ 47c7557a-fd4c-5c59-a05c-f5fed2da4136.html.

"9th Annual Chair-Ity Event." OMCAR, OMCAR's Young Professionals Network, 2016, www.omcar.com/events1/annual-chair-ity-event/.

"Cooking Up Dreams." Family Service Agency, Family Service Agency, 2017, fsacares.org/cooking-up-dreams/.

Appendix A

Timeline of Fundraising Events

ASAP:

- Assign members of your group to head up committee for food, decorations, sponsors, advertising, ticket sales, and setup/cleanup. Have members volunteer for committees and ask the committees to meet regularly and report back to the group.

- Determine your budget — know how much money you need to raise and how much you can spend on the event.

- Decide on the date for the event. Try to avoid conflicts with any other community events, especially if they are likely to overshadow your own.

- Find sponsors. Include their names or logos on all advertising and link to them on social media.

Four Months Before Event:

- If food will be served, plan the menu. Schedule a caterer or arrange for volunteer cooks. Ask restaurants or stores to donate food.

- Line up entertainment (auctioneer, MC, band, etc.)

Three Months Before Event:

- Create an event theme, graphics, or color scheme to use in all marketing.

- Create an event on social media and invite everyone you know. Send an email invitation. Post flyers at school and around town. Contact local newspapers and radio stations to request publicity.

- Set up a mechanism for ticket sales — either online or in person through your members.

- Arrange for any special equipment like sound systems, lighting, or stage equipment.

One Month Before Event:

- Walk-through the venue to plan your setup and check to make sure all sound and lighting systems work. Ask when you can get in to decorate.

- Write a script to serve as your minute-by-minute flow of activities for the event's MC. Be sure to include thanking your sponsors.

- Have a meeting for all event volunteers to make sure everyone knows their job, schedule, and what to wear. Be sure to get everyone's contact information so you can communicate changes and reminders.

Appendix B
Pledge Form for Potential Sponsors

It's time for [**Organization Name**]'s
[**Year**] [**Event**]!
[**Day of the week**], [**Date**] [**Time**]
[**Place**]

Dear Potential Sponsor,

I, [Name] am participating in the [**Organization Name**] [activity]. All proceeds will help fund [**list of activities**]. You can sponsor me for a specific amount and can name a maximum amount that you are willing to contribute. After the [**activity**], I will inform you of what I did and collect your contribution. Please make checks payable to [**Organization Name**]. All contributions are tax-deductible.

Thank you!

Sponsor	Pledge (Example: $1.00 per lap)	Maximum Pledge	Amount Collected	Business Matching Pledge Amount

Participants:

To reach our goal, we hope that each participant finds 15 sponsors.

Please bring this form to our meeting on the day of the event, [**Day of the week**], [**Date**].

Double Your Contribution

The following is a list of employers who will match employees' contributions. Please ask everyone who sponsors you if his or her employer is on this list.

[Company Name]	[Company Name]	[Company Name]
[Company Name]	[Company Name]	[Company Name]
[Company Name]	[Company Name]	[Company Name]

Appendix C
Rules for Participants Collecting Pledges

Annual [**Organization Name**]
[**Year**] [**Event**]!
[**Day of the week**], [**Date**]

Our annual event is [description of event]

Our goal is to help [organization name] raise at least $[amount] to fund [list of activities]. We hope that each participant in the event contributes to the best of his/her ability. If each participant raises $[amount], we will achieve our goal. We're hoping to make this event the best ever, so the more contributions you raise, the more successful we'll be at achieving our goal. Thank you for your participation.

Rules

1. Participants may start collecting pledges as soon as they receive the pledge sheets. **Reminder: Pledge sheets need to be turned in on event day, [Day of the week], [Date].**

2. Pledges may be made by anyone. However, participants may not ask for pledges from any of the staff members of [**Organization Name**]. **Please ask everyone who pledges if his/her company has**

a matching gift fund policy. Companies who match pledge gifts are listed on the back of the pledge sheet.

3. **Each sponsor making a pledge should write his/her name, pledge, and maximum pledge.** Students may collect the pledge in advance but must keep pledges until all are collected.

4. On the event day, each participant will be issued a summary of his/her participation, which will be the participant record of the event.

5. Upon completion of the event, participants will hand in their summaries. A volunteer will record each person's participation on the pledge sheet and return it. Participants may then collect outstanding pledges. **Please return pledge sheets with the money to [Organization Name] by [Day of the week], [Date] to [location].**

6. Participants are encouraged to dress appropriately for the event. Bring a hat and sunscreen if the weather is anticipated to be sunny, or bring rain gear if the weather is expected to be overcast.

We look forward to all our participants having a great time! For questions or concerns, or to volunteer, contact **[Coordinator] at [phone number] or [e-mail address].**

Auto
diagnostic
amoureux

Infographie : Johanne Lemay
Révision : Élyse-Andrée Héroux

DISTRIBUTEURS EXCLUSIFS :

Pour le Canada et les États-Unis :
MESSAGERIES ADP*
2315, rue de la Province
Longueuil, Québec J4G 1G4
Téléphone : 450 640-1237
Télécopieur : 450 674-6237
Internet : www.messageries-adp.com
* filiale du Groupe Sogides inc.,
  filiale de Quebecor Media inc.

Pour la France et les autres pays :
INTERFORUM editis
Immeuble Paryseine, 3, Allée de la Seine
94854 Ivry CEDEX
Téléphone : 33 (0) 1 49 59 11 56/91
Télécopieur : 33 (0) 1 49 59 11 33
Service commandes France Métropolitaine
Téléphone : 33 (0) 2 38 32 71 00
Télécopieur : 33 (0) 2 38 32 71 28
Internet : www.interforum.fr
Service commandes Export – DOM-TOM
Télécopieur : 33 (0) 2 38 32 78 86
Internet : www.interforum.fr
Courriel : cdes-export@interforum.fr

Pour la Suisse :
INTERFORUM editis SUISSE
Case postale 69 – CH 1701 Fribourg – Suisse
Téléphone : 41 (0) 26 460 80 60
Télécopieur : 41 (0) 26 460 80 68
Internet : www.interforumsuisse.ch
Courriel : office@interforumsuisse.ch
Distributeur : OLF S.A.
ZI. 3, Corminboeuf
Case postale 1061 – CH 1701 Fribourg – Suisse
Commandes :
Téléphone : 41 (0) 26 467 53 33
Télécopieur : 41 (0) 26 467 54 66
Internet : www.olf.ch
Courriel : information@olf.ch

Pour la Belgique et le Luxembourg :
INTERFORUM BENELUX S.A.
Fond Jean-Pâques, 6
B-1348 Louvain-La-Neuve
Téléphone : 32 (0) 10 42 03 20
Télécopieur : 32 (0) 10 41 20 24
Internet : www.interforum.be
Courriel : info@interforum.be

Gouvernement du Québec – Programme de crédit
d'impôt pour l'édition de livres – Gestion SODEC –
www.sodec.gouv.qc.ca

L'Éditeur bénéficie du soutien de la Société de dével-
oppement des entreprises culturelles du Québec
pour son programme d'édition.

Conseil des Arts   Canada Council
du Canada   for the Arts

Nous remercions le Conseil des Arts du Canada de
l'aide accordée à notre programme de publication.

Nous reconnaissons l'aide financière du gouvernement du Canada par l'entremise du Fonds du livre
du Canada pour nos activités d'édition.